BRANDENBURG-PR

Studies in European History

Series Editors: John Breuilly
Julian Jackson
Peter Wilson

Jeremy Black	*A Military Revolution? Military Change and European Society, 1550–1800*
T.C.W. Blanning	*The French Revolution: Class War or Culture Clash?* (2nd edn)
John Breuilly	*The Formation of the First German Nation-State, 1800–1871*
Peter Burke	*The Renaissance* (2nd edn)
Michael L. Dockrill and Michael F. Hopkins	*The Cold War 1945–1991* (2nd edn)
William Doyle	*The Ancien Régime* (2nd edn)
William Doyle	*Jansenism*
Andy Durgan	*The Spanish Civil War*
Geoffrey Ellis	*The Napoleonic Empire* (2nd edn)
Donald A. Filtzer	*The Krushchev Era*
Karin Friedrich	*Bandenburg-Prussia, 1466–1806*
Mary Fulbrook	*Interpretations of the Two Germanies, 1945–1990* (2nd edn)
Graeme Gill	*Stalinism* (2nd edn)
Hugh Gough	*The Terror in the French Revolution* (2nd edn)
Peter Grieder	*The German Democratic Republic*
John Henry	*The Scientific Revolution and the Origins of Modern Science* (3rd edn)
Stefan-Ludwig Hoffmann	*Civil Society, 1750–1914*
Henry Kamen	*Golden Age Spain* (2nd edn)
Richard Mackenney	*The City-State, 1500–1700*
Andrew Porter	*European Imperialism, 1860–1914*
Roy Porter	*The Enlightenment* (2nd edn)
Roger Price	*The Revolutions of 1848*
James Retallack	*Germany in the Age of Kaiser Wilhelm II*
Richard Sakwa	*Communism in Russia*
Geoffrey Scarre and John Callow	*Witchcraft and Magic in 16th- and 17th-Century Europe* (2nd edn)
R.W. Scribner and C. Scott Dixon	*The German Reformation* (2nd edn)
Robert Service	*The Russian Revolution, 1900–1927* (4th edn)
Jeremy Smith	*The Fall of Soviet Communism, 1985–1991*
David Stevenson	*The Outbreak of the First World War*
Peter H. Wilson	*The Holy Roman Empire, 1495–1806* (2nd edn)
Oliver Zimmer	*Nationalism in Europe, 1890–1940*

**Studies in European History
Series Standing Order
ISBN 0–333–79365–X**
(*outside North America only*)

You can receive future titles in this series as they are published by placing a standing order. Please contact your bookseller or, in case of difficulty, write to us at the address below with your name and address, the title of the series and the ISBN quoted above.
Customer Services Department, Macmillan Distribution Ltd
Houndmilis, Basingstoke, Hampshire RG21 6XS, England

Introduction

and Baltic peoples, between Pagans, Catholics, Protestants, the Orthodox and Jews. Much of the more recent historiography presented here showcases this pluralism, embodied in estate assemblies, provincial legal traditions, institutions and identities, which the Hohenzollern dynasty tried to harmonise partly in open conflict, partly through cooperation with its composite elites. Owing to its character as a collection of territories joined in a dynastic, personal union, much of older Brandenburg-Prussian history has been written as a history of forceful rulers, eminent soldiers and philosopher-kings, and the centralised state they were credited with building. From the myth attached to the Great Elector Frederick William as the 'founder of the Prussian state', to Frederick the Great, contradictory voices have been few and far between. Ernest Lavisse stressed this in 1891, when he wrote that Prussia did not exist either as a race or as a geographical region, and had been created not by nature but by man [92, 35].

The purpose of this study, however, is not mainly to chart the dynasty's success in forging a unitary Prussian state, but to focus on the vitality of its composite parts and their constructive, modernising potential. This only makes sense if neighbouring, east-central European traditions of non-absolute, mixed forms of government (particularly that of Poland-Lithuania) are recognised as models which crucially influenced Prussian developments. An attempt within English-language historiography to relocate Brandenburg-Prussia in the context of this region's constitutional and composite traditions to which it belonged – before its defeat by Napoleon in 1806/7, its reconstitution at the Congress of Vienna, and its subsequent westward expansion in the early nineteenth century created a different playing field – is long overdue.

One of the questions which threads itself through the first part of this book is therefore why the provincial estate assemblies and elites abandoned their cherished liberties of self-government [79] and accepted their dynastic rulers' integrationist programme, although different parts of the agglomeration chose different speeds and intensities of integration. The 'rise of absolutism', which has often been associated with this development, has come under much attack over the last twenty years. Yet when a new generation of historians of France challenged the nature of Louis XIV's 'absolute' monarchy in the 1980s from a provincial perspective, Prussian 'absolutism' survived this historiographical onslaught practically unscathed [103].

Several German historians have stressed the 'non-absolutist within absolutism', but they found it hard to alter Anglo-Saxon views of Prussian absolutism, despite pointing out that representative bodies of the estates continued in some territories on a local basis even though their central assemblies no longer existed [59, 27, 131]. The consensus now is that so-called absolute rulers did not build a modern state in a purposeful, systematic and structured way [113], but in response to the necessities and emergencies that arose from the composite nature of Brandenburg-Prussian politics.

It is also time to dismantle some of the older assumptions on the governmental and institutional structures of the Prussian state – assumptions that were first spread as enlightened propaganda by Prussian bureaucrats themselves and reiterated by historians, who after the chaos of two world wars in the twentieth century quite understandably embraced Prussia's myth of orderly and efficient centralisation. The growing influence of cultural and anthropological approaches has helped in the dismantling of this myth. In a reaction against a misunderstood Hegelian idea of the state and Weber's concept of modern sovereignty, a new cultural history of politics has queried the assertion that political structures are objective 'givens' rather than circumstances created by social and cultural practices and historically negotiated norms. Some historians even question the assumed essence of the state: 'It only exists because one speaks about it ... one mustn't discuss *that* it existed but only *how* it existed' [91]. Hence the nature of Prussian absolute government cannot merely be derived from centrally passed edicts and ordinances but must be perceived through a large range of cultural and political practices which supported or opposed such a style of government, often only held together by a common title or office, while policy-makers expressedly admitted a variety of strategies and approaches in different parts of the composite state [75].

Interest in the provincial level, in the 'little people' and in history 'from below' has been late and slow to come to historians of Prussia. During the Cold War, Klaus Zernack argued in vain that regional and local perspectives needed to be recognised when writing the history of Brandenburg-Prussia [43]. Since the fall of the wall in 1989 several weighty volumes on the territories of Mark Brandenburg, Altmark, Uckermark and Prignitz have emerged, with a focus on social and micro-history which have opened new perspectives on Brandenburg-Prussia's composite territories [184, 22]. The legacy

Introduction

of the non-Germans in Prussia, however, still suffers neglect, only partly due to language barriers. The main reason until recently was the tendency to categorise Prussian history above all as the history of a 'German' dynasty [9]. Most histories of Prussia therefore start with (and concentrate on) the history of Brandenburg, as the heartland of Hohenzollern power from the fifteenth century [17, 3]. The publication in 1994 and 1996 of a German textbook on East and West Prussia tried to address this problem through a co-production of German and Polish authors, but ultimately disappoints, since it only includes two token historians from Poland, while most chapters ignore Polish historical works on the subject [29].

In contrast, this study tries to emphasise the importance of Ducal or Eastern Prussia for the development of the whole Brandenburg-Prussian state and gives a voice to the rich tradition of Polish historical research on this province. This book's narrative starts in the east, with the first chapter focusing on the history of the legacy of the Teutonic Knights in Prussia, the province which gave Brandenburg-Prussia its name and eventually an identity. The success of its Hohenzollern rulers who, after secularising the Teutonic state as a fief of the Polish crown, claimed the prize of hereditary succession as dukes in Prussia in 1618 and of sovereignty in 1657, gave Brandenburg the opportunity to conduct policies independent from the strictures of the Holy Roman Empire. The second chapter tries to gauge the relationship between the theory and practice of 'state-building', including its all-important confessional aspects. There is often a separation of political history and religious developments in older works on Brandenburg-Prussia, which usually summarised the disparity between a Calvinist rulership from 1613 and a Lutheran population under the heading of Prussian toleration. This study does not introduce a separate chapter on religion for the reason that religious and political practices were closely intertwined in the multi-confessional territories of Brandenburg-Prussia; hence the history of religious conflict is one of the threads that run through the whole book. This chapter also familiarises readers with important revisions in recent historiography addressing Büsch's theory of Brandenburg-Prussia's 'social militarisation', which generations of historians welcomed as a coherent explanation for a Prusso-German *Sonderweg*.

New historiographical impulses on the history of social relationships in the countryside are discussed in chapter 3, which focuses on the rural economy and the political power of the nobility and its subjects within a great variety of territorial contexts. The fourth chapter, on the Prussian court, is inspired by the new cultural history of politics. Both the court and the military were deeply influenced by ritual and symbolic practice, an area which has rarely been explored with regard to Brandenburg-Prussia. Chapter 5 on foreign policy examines Brandenburg-Prussia in a dual context, between its orientation towards the Holy Roman Empire on the one hand, and north-eastern Europe on the other. Finally, much has been made of the Prussian Enlightenment, its roots in Pietism, cameralism and educational reform, but also in the utilitarian rationalism of Christian Wolff (1679–1754). The contradictions of enlightened absolutism will be discussed with particular reference to Prussian toleration of Huguenots, Jews and Catholics, and linked with the emergence of an enlightened public sphere during Frederick II's reign. This public sphere stimulated the broader reception of enlightened ideas but remained within the defined limits of obedience to a monarchy which refused to become constitutional.

Most histories of Prussia speculate on the many near-deaths and disasters the country survived. The book ends on the threshold between pre-modern and modern times, when the wars against revolutionary and Napoleonic France brought the destruction of the Holy Roman Empire – Brandenburg's political home for so many centuries – and almost caused Prussia's disintegration. It is best to stop there – not only because the ancien régime had come to an end to be replaced by modern ideas of nationhood and liberalism, but also because the reforms of the early nineteenth century propelled the country into a new age. There are, however, also continuities. After Prussia's recovery as a member of the pentarchy of European great powers, its rulers continued to build on the negative alliance with the Russian Empire against an occupied and partitioned Poland. The antagonisms between Prussians, Germans and Poles were determined by these new power structures until another Empire came to an end, destroyed by national ambition between 1914 and 1918.

1 The Teutonic Legacy

[i] Origins

In the eastern marshes of the Baltic coast, in the early thirteenth century, the Order of the Teutonic Knights began to create a formidable military and administrative organisation, subjugating the local pagan population and building a network of castles and towns. Almost two hundred years later, at the epic battle of Grunwald/Tannenberg in 1410, the combined Polish and Lithuanian forces under King Władysław Jagiełło (Jogaila) and his cousin Witold (Vytautas) wiped out the elite of the Teutonic Knights. This defeat not only ended the myth of the Teutonic Knights' invincibility; it signalled a century of decline in the Teutonic Order's fortunes in Prussia and the southern Baltic. By 1466 they had lost control of the western Prussian lands, including Danzig, to the Poles, and in 1525, after a series of lost wars that had followed Tannenberg, the Order's last grand master, Albrecht of Hohenzollern, secularised the Teutonic state. He transformed it into a hereditary duchy, submitting himself as a vassal to the king of Poland and ruling the duchy as a fief of the Polish crown.

The reasons for these developments are manifold. The power and reputation of the Teutonic Knights had been on the wane for some time. Crusading in the Baltic was losing its appeal for the German noblemen who had formerly flocked to join the Order. Lithuania, the last pagan bastion of north-eastern Europe, had fallen when Grand Duke Jogaila accepted Catholicism (not Orthodox Christianity, the religion of his Slavic subjects in Lithuania) on his marriage with Jadwiga, queen of Poland, in 1386. Nobles and cities under the Order's control increasingly resented the rule by an ecclesiastical and military elite which siphoned off economic gains through monopolies and prevented their subjects from gaining greater political and legal autonomy over their own affairs. All of these factors contributed to the decline of a once sophisticated, economically flourishing and highly organised military power [49, 44].

This medieval heritage was of great significance for the future development of Brandenburg-Prussia. The Baltic roots were just as important, if not more so, for the future development of the early modern composite state, as this inheritance ultimately gave the electors of Brandenburg a unique advantage over their rival German princes whose influence and lands were restricted to the Empire. The Prussian legacy enabled the early modern electorate to elevate its status to monarchy in 1701 and build a network of territories that was to dominate Germany in the nineteenth century. Although Prussia's native Baltic population was conquered and dominated by a German elite, the influence of non-German populations on Prussia's development was still considerable. This chapter is based on recent research exploring the complex origins of Prussia in a society that was to a large extent colonial and multi-ethnic, but possessed its own distinct legal and political traditions. It will also look at Teutonic Prussia's legacy for the later history of the state's composite character, its function as a borderland between Germans, Baltic peoples and Slavs, and its role in Central Europe.

In the last three decades, in Germany, Poland and to a lesser extent in the English-speaking world, the picture of the Teutonic Knights has undergone considerable change. From the end of the fifteenth century, when the Polish chronicles described the battle of Tannenberg as a fight between equals of great and noble origin, to the National Socialists, who so cynically instrumentalised history for their brutal expansion into Eastern Europe, and to the post-1945 period, when the Teutonic 'push towards the East' was depicted as a 'Western imperialist' design on Poland and the Eastern bloc, the symbolism attached to the Teutonic Order was always a powerful propaganda tool in the shared history of Germans and Poles.

It is well worth remembering that the identification of the Teutonic Knights with the German nation is a product of the modern age. Although in the fourteenth and fifteenth centuries the Teutonic Order became one of Poland's main enemies, it did not prevent considerable Polish military contingents to take part in battles on the Teutonic side. Moreover, Polish and Lithuanian rulers did not hesitate to conclude alliances with the Teutonic Knights when it suited them. It was only in the early nineteenth century that a new, romantic nationalism, heralded during the wars of liberation against Napoleon, redefined the legacy of the Teutonic Order. Literary works, such as Joseph von Eichendorff's *The Last Hero of Marienburg* (1830), emphasised the continuity between the Order's heroic past and the kingdom of Prussia. The negative image of the Order lived on in the drama *Konrad Wallenrod* (1828), by Poland's most famous romantic poet, Adam Mickiewicz. A propagandistic battle over the Teutonic past followed between Treitschke's stirring call in 1862 for Otto von Bismarck to take up the traditions of the Knights to create a German great power in Europe, and the publication of Henryk Sienkiewicz's novel *The Teutonic Knights* (1897–1900) on the Polish side [56, 57]. The inherent irony that the Teutonic Order remained a Catholic force, supported by the Pope and the Catholic House of Habsburg throughout the centuries, did not prevent the subsequent instrumentalisation of its symbolism by the Protestant Prussian dynasty: Emperor William II presented himself surrounded with mock-Teutonic Knights and dressed in historic costume at Marienburg castle to celebrate the accomplished reconstruction of the fortress in 1902.

After the German defeat in the First World War, the restitution of a Polish state in 1918, and the creation of the Danzig corridor, the forceful propagation of the 'Teutonic domination of the East' continued unabated. During the Weimar and Nazi periods, highly politicised historians, geographers and ethnologists developed the discipline of German *Ostforschung*, which argued the racial, cultural, political and economic superiority of 'Germandom' in Eastern Europe, legitimising territorial expansion and occupation [50]. The Polish response followed in the form of *Westforschung*, which sought evidence for the autochthonous origins of the Slavic population in Prussia, Silesia and Pomerania. The history of colonisation under the Teutonic Order thus regained enormous political significance, a situation which was only exacerbated after 1945, when Polish historians had to justify the shunting of the Polish state westward after the Treaty of Yalta and the consequent expulsion of large numbers of German inhabitants from Prussia and Silesia. The communist regime in Poland exploited the anti-Polish thrust of the Order's nationalist image to keep its own population in a state of fear over the (West) German aggressor. The partly Marxist, partly nationalist concept of a Polish-dominated *Pomorze* (land on the sea), which embraced most of the southern Baltic coast from Pomerania to the modern Lithuanian border, blurred the distinction between territories divided by considerable differences in origin and allegiance [7, 36].

After the fall of communism and the unification of Germany, the task of a new generation of scholars across the Polish–German border was to deconstruct such ideological traditions. Since 1990 an increasingly sophisticated historiography on the Teutonic period in Prussia has evolved, which has also begun to penetrate schoolbooks, a process prepared by the German-Polish textbook commission established in 1972, which brought slow but irreversible changes to the relationship between Polish and German historians of Prussia [369].

[ii] A Colonial Society

Until the fateful battle of Tannenberg in 1410, the Teutonic Order was a well-organised, strictly hierarchical medieval corporation that controlled a feared military force [49]. The Knights ruled the Prussian lands from five main castle districts: Christburg, Osterode, Elbing, Balga, Brandenburg and Königsberg (see Map 2 and Gazetteer). Within those districts, a number of local governors overlooked the major administrative units of the Order, the *Komtureien* (commanderies). From 1309 the Order's main seat was the castle in Marienburg. Yet the number of Knights active in Prussia was never large. Just before 1410, historians estimate that around 700 men belonged to the Teutonic Order as knights, including the grand master and the Komturs, who were its chief officers, but excluding lower administrative officials.

The population under the Order's rule was divided by substantial differences in legal and social status, descent, culture and language. The most important factor shaping the colonisation of the country was not just the influx of settlers from the Holy Roman Empire and western parts of Europe, but the often neglected fact that the native Pruzzen population survived and was augmented by Polish and Lithuanian colonists. Although numbers are hard to establish, it is estimated that in 1400 approximately 140,000 Pruzzen, 103,000 settlers, principally from the German lands and Flanders, and 270,000 Poles, Kaszubs (a Slavic population with a language related to Polish) and Lithuanians lived there [47].

These populations did not mingle easily, mainly due to the legal and economic boundaries between them, set up and maintained by the Order's authorities [40]. Settlers who originated from German territories in the Empire received privileges based on Kulm law, a mixture of Magdeburg law and other German, Flemish and customary law traditions. It was the grand master Hermann von Salza who granted the first charters to the city of Kulm (Chełmno) and Thorn (Toruń) in 1233. The Kulm constitutions applied to towns, nobles and the countryside alike and regulated the relationship between the Teutonic Order and its subjects.

Initially, this law favoured urban society and guaranteed personal freedom to the settlers from the German lands. Nobles, however, disliked the law's inheritance rules, which gave female and male lines equal rights [58]. The division of property among children threatened many noble families with long-term impoverishment. By introducing equal inheritance among male children, the Teutonic Knights ensured that neither the local Pruzzen, nor German and Polish nobles became rich and powerful enough to rise into a position of economic competition with them. The majority of the land remained under the administration and ownership of the Teutonic Order. Most lands were leased out on emphyteutic tenures to free peasants, so-called *Zinsbauern*, who paid quit rent in return, maintained fortifications and castles nearby, or fulfilled other moderate labour services for the Order, usually restricted to a few days per year [2].

After the first wave of immigration, the fourteenth century saw a massive fall in the number of new colonists. Yet colonisation in the easternmost lands of the Teutonic Order continued with the help of settlers from the duchy of Pomerania, Brandenburg, Lusatia, and other territories in the German–Slavic borderlands, along the rivers Elbe, Drewenz, Oder, Pregel and Nogat. The colonists moved further east, to the River Memel and into what later became Prussian Lithuania [53]. Slowly, towns developed into trade centres. Their economy did not only boost local exchange but, in most cases, also transcended the Prussian borders through regular trade contacts with Poland (especially Mazovia, Great Poland and Cujavia) and Pomerania, even in times of war (see Maps 1 and 2). Polish migrants from the duchy of Mazovia, which had close relations with the Teutonic Order, settled in the eastern area of the Mazurian lakes (east of Warmia), attracted by Kulm law privileges, including fishing rights in the teeming lakes, and promises of tax privileges. These arrangements helped the relatively swift colonisation of the

Prussian wilderness. Karol Górski's classic verdict that the Order was a 'quasi-colonial' power still rings true today, even if his thesis that the Order only admitted people of German origin to its hierarchy has since been revised [124].

Differences in the legal traditions applied to settlers and native populations provided an efficient instrument of discrimination. The Baltic Pruzzen, though not 'exterminated', as older historical interpretations suggested, were treated most harshly. Of all groups, they were the most disadvantaged and did not even possess the status of a legal person, although individuals served alongside nobles of German or Slavic origin in the army and played a crucial role in the colonisation of the land [45]. After several unsuccessful attempts to mount armed rebellions against the Teutonic occupation of their territories, they were settled in separate villages (*Hakendörfer*). Over time, most Pruzzen peasants became bound to the soil and usually lived as cottagers, gardeners or servants, often employed in the castles and Komtureien. They lost their freedom of movement and property, received smaller plots of land to work on than German peasants, were taxed more heavily and had to provide more labour duties.

Still, those who were able to purchase their freedom could leave and take their moveable property with them. With the transformation of many Pruzzen villages into Kulm law settlements in the fourteenth century, some gained personal freedom [2; 69]. The most successful Pruzzen served in the light infantry of the Teutonic Order and were thus able to assume lowly offices in the territorial administrative hierarchy and mix with German or Polish nobles. They did this with greater ease than the Teutonic authorities would have liked, as is shown by repeated decrees aimed at preventing mixed settlements. A contemporary warning read: 'Those who want to found German villages have to ensure that they do not settle any Pruzzen in a German village' and that 'if a Pruzzen servant is found in a German settlement, the highest court will prosecute them' [31; 126].

Few historians have picked up on Henryk Łowmiański's thesis, that it might well have been thanks to the Teutonic Order's interference that the Pruzzen population preserved its social, cultural and legal structures as long as it did by escaping the forces of assimilation with the Slavic population and the influence of Polish law, as happened in medieval Pomerania, under the local Slavic dynasty [53; 453]. As a result of this conscious policy of discrimination, the Pruzzen population was also able to hold on to their pagan beliefs.

The Teutonic Legacy

Due to a shortage of adequately trained priests, the Lithuanian and Pruzzen population in eastern Prussia suffered from a severe neglect of religious care. Mass was said with the assistance of translators, who helped the local – often barely literate – parish priest to communicate with the Baltic population, many of whom continued their pagan rituals down to the Reformation and beyond. The chronicler Matthäus Prätorius (1635–1707), who collected knowledge of the Lithuanian language and relied on oral testimonies, heard reports from parish clergy who complained about the longevity of pagan traditions [364].

Between 1410 and the devastating Thirteen Years War (1454–66), a last and important wave of immigration, encouraged by the Order, tried to rebuild wrecked villages and areas in eastern Prussia. In contrast to Livonia and Courland, where an exclusively German noble elite continued to dominate an indigenous Baltic peasant society, in fourteenth- and fifteenth-century Prussia the German, Polish and Pruzzen population became more integrated and socially mobile; as Francis Carsten observed, 'in the country as a whole, the German immigrants were a minority' [2; 71].

The picture was similar in the territories of Pomerelia, near the mouth of the River Vistula, which the Order occupied in 1308–9. Here, the burghers and nobles and their Slavic rulers had appealed to the Knights for help against the margrave of Brandenburg, who had tried to conquer their province. Yet after driving out the Brandenburgers, the Knights stayed. In the 1343 treaty of Kalisz, Pomerelia was officially ceded to the Knights, including the lands of Kulm and Michelau, which were confirmed as Teutonic possessions (see Map 2). Pomerania and Pomerelia had been Christianised in the tenth century and did not need the zeal of the Teutonic Order to convert them to the Christian church. In fact, the Pomeranian rulers fought the triple threat from pagan Pruzzen raids, the Teutonic Knights from the East, and the ambitious Brandenburg Ascanian rulers in the south-west. Successful urban centres, such as Danzig, had been founded before the Teutonic conquest. Pomerelia was clearly the most urbanised part of the Order's lands, with 25 per cent of the population living in towns and cities, whereas in the eastern Prussian regions only one-fifth of the population lived in urban centres. In Pomerelia, the Polish and Kaszub population formed the majority and eventually served the Order as loyal subjects, holding land and following their own Polish law traditions. Even after their conquest by the Teutonic Order, the districts and regions along the Vistula and its delta remained under the authority of the Polish bishoprics of Gniezno (in Great Poland) and Włocławek (in Cujavia).

In contrast to other German–Slavic borderlands, the settlement of colonists in the Order's state had been strictly regulated, which meant that control over landed property remained mainly in the hands of the Teutonic Knights. As a result, the Prussian landowning nobility were not particularly wealthy. Above all, the nobility resented that their status was not recognised, as Prussian secular nobles were merely accorded the title of 'major' or 'minor' freemen, despite serving in armour. This refusal by the Order to acknowledge nobility outside its own organisation nourished resentment among the Prussian estates and forged an easy alliance between nobles and patricians – a development which was later to prove fatal for the Teutonic Knights' rule over Prussia. During the fifteenth century, Prussian society became more aware of its common interests: more than anything else, it was the resistance against the Order that led to a more united 'Prussian identity' in the age of the Renaissance.

[iii] The Idea of Prussia and the Development of Representative Bodies

It was foreign observers and visitors who first transferred the name of the original inhabitants, the Pruzzen, to the Teutonic Knights (*Pruteni*) and their Order (*ordo Prutenorum*): the Order of the Prussians. In the second half of the fifteenth century, Pope Pius II – who had travelled across Prussia and Lithuania before being elevated to the papacy – called the original Pruzzen inhabitants 'non-baptised Prussians'. It is difficult to establish exactly what identity was by then associated with the name of Prussia and Prussians. Immatriculation records of the sons of Prussian nobles and patricians at European universities show that as early as the fifteenth century their signatures included 'de Prussia' or 'Prutenus' (Prussian) to indicate their origin [54]. Local political leaders in the towns and the non-Teutonic nobility no longer considered themselves immigrants, but inhabitants of the lands of Prussia, and therefore Prussians.

Similarly indicative of the newly developing identification with Prussia are chronicles on the country's history, from its pagan origins in a mythical past, to a political history written by scholars increasingly critical of the Teutonic Knights' own hagiographic tradition. One of the first outspoken critics of the Order was the priest Johann von Posilge (1340–1418), from a Pruzzen family near Marienburg, who wrote a secular history of the people, customs and society in the lands of Prussia. Anti-Teutonic works also emanated from the monastery of Oliva, near Danzig, and the Franciscan Order in Thorn [33, 37]. The increasingly confident use of works by ancient authors, especially Tacitus, which helped to glorify the political independence of the Baltic pagan tribes of the past, stood in growing contrast to the Rome-oriented and self-centred chronicles of the Order.

Mounting tensions between the Knights and their subjects served as the catalyst for the evolution of the idea of a Prussia that was independent from and even hostile to the Teutonic Order. Informal assemblies of representatives from the cities, inspired by the corporate bodies of the Hanseatic League, became institutionalised centres of resistance [124]. Between 1230 and 1410, the Prussian cities took part in numerous Hanseatic assemblies and in the League's wars against Denmark. They also discussed the defence of their interests against the Order. Following the example of the politically more vociferous cities, the landed nobility finally rallied to the cause in 1397 and founded the so-called Lizard League in Kulm. With Lithuania's Christianisation and dynastic union with Poland in 1386, the main reason for the Order's original mission – the conversion of pagans – had disappeared. It was after this event that the estates mustered increasing courage to present their grievances. The first written complaints of nobles and burghers against the Order's tax and war policies go back to the years 1388–93 [58; 131–48].

After the Order's disastrous defeat at Tannenberg in 1410, the Prussian cities sent representatives to Marienburg castle to enter into concrete negotiations with the Polish king, Władysław Jagiełło. He promised to remedy all their grievances and to grant them extensive privileges if Prussia joined the crown of Poland. This enhanced the estates' bargaining powers. It was above all the cities that resisted any diminution of economic and legal privileges guaranteed in their Kulm law charters. Urban self-government had existed several decades before the nobility built up similar corporate bodies and strengthened the country's resistance against the

Teutonic Order's monopoly of power. In 1440, the nobles and cities joined together to form the Prussian League. This body, immediately outlawed by the Order, launched a rebellion of that was to bring about the partitioning of Prussia between 1454 and 1466.

The negative picture of the Teutonic Order's oppressive policies against the cities, aggravated by a deep economic crisis in the first half of the fifteenth century, has recently been challenged. Although the tight territorial organisation of the Teutonic state originally delayed the emergence of self-government, the growth of urban autonomy, especially in Hanseatic towns such as Danzig, Elbing, Thorn or Königsberg after 1400 was rapid and intense. Prussian cities successfully gained trade privileges, extended their jurisdictional rights, kept taxes down and reduced the number of armed men called up to contribute to the Order's wars. The city councils even sought to take over the election and appointment procedures for the creation of magistrates. Trades and crafts flourished through co-operation between the Order's trade agents, their craftsmen, and the Prussian cities, and were not as universally characterised by hostile competition from the Order as formerly suspected [51].

The Teutonic Knights enabled the patriciate in the larger cities to meet other Hanseatic towns at international gatherings and organise their trade contacts relatively freely. Rarely did the Knights intrude in internal conflicts within the cities. The magistrates and merchant elites benefited from the reluctance of the Prussian nobility to enter into any closer agreement with the Teutonic Knights or to join forces with them against the cities. Following military and diplomatic defeats, the Order had to turn more frequently to the rich patriciate of Danzig to borrow money. This development not only strengthened the cities' confidence and bolstered local identity; it also established a systematic policy of cooperation and solidarity among the cities, including the weaker and smaller towns.

One question remains, however: why, if the Order's policies and economic activities did not particularly hurt or disadvantage the Prussian towns' development, did the patriciate by the mid-fifteenth century turn against their Teutonic masters so relatively unanimously? Most protests were directed not against systematic chicanery by the Order, but against specific officials who abused their powers by forcing merchants to sell their wares more cheaply, hindering export, using violence and breaking established laws. The main bone of contention between the Order and its subjects was the attempt to introduce new taxes and custom tariffs to cover the rapidly growing costs of mercenary armies for the wars against Poland–Lithuania (after the drying up of military volunteers from the 1390s), and to compensate for the inadequate income from landed estates during a period of economic crisis [55].

The greatest profits for the Knights came from the so-called *Pfundgeld*, which was originally levelled by the Hanseatic League on the weight of goods transferred from and into Hanseatic ports in the mid-fourteenth century, and had then been administered by the Prussian cities themselves. In 1403, the Order decided to refashion these tolls into a regular tariff collected for the Knights' coffers. By 1409 two-thirds of this tariff, owed by merchants in Prussian Hanseatic cities, flowed into the Teutonic treasury. By 1434, the grand master declared the tariff a general territorial tax and tried to requisition the whole amount. The economic loss to the cities could not have been overwhelming, as they waited until 1453 to present complaints against the *Pfundzoll*; but it was the principle rather than the tariff itself which rankled [51; 206].

Relations between the Teutonic Order and the city of Danzig had deteriorated particularly rapidly after 1410. The Danzig *Chronicle of the League* complained bitterly about the duplicity of the Order which had 'invited Danzig burghers to dine with them, but killed and murdered them instead, deprived many of their property, raped and killed their wives and daughters' [52; 411]. This was not only in breach of the privileges confirmed by the Teutonic Knights themselves, but seriously undermined the Order's reputation. Such clashes between the cities and the Prussian assemblies defending their self-government on the one hand, and the Teutonic Order, demanding full authority as territorial ruler on the other, were not dissimilar to power struggles between territorial rulers and corporate bodies elsewhere in Renaissance Europe.

While the cities' identity as members of the Hanseatic League diminished with the decline of this international organisation, they pooled their interests with the nobility in regular estate assemblies, so-called *Tagfahrten*. This happened later than in Brandenburg or Pomerania, where the estates had developed regular representative assemblies and diets by the end of the thirteenth century, or in Poland, where representative institutions emerged after the Polish–Lithuanian union of 1386, and the king granted the privilege of *neminem captivabimus*, a stronger version of the English principle of *habeas corpus*. Still, the Prussian estates embodied what Górski called 'a prime example of a natural development of representative institutions'. Moreover, they formulated a comprehensive theory of resistance [124; 29]. It was put to the test in 1432: when the grand master, despite a valid peace treaty, declared war on Poland, the nobility of the Kulm lands refused to raise arms and cross the Polish border, and the Prussian cities boycotted a common council with the Teutonic Knights.

It was the formation of the Prussian League, initiated by the cities in 1440, that opened the last chapter of the long story of the rule of the Teutonic Knights over Prussia. From the 1420s, the Prussian cities no longer sent representatives to Hanseatic assemblies. A new generation had grown up which had not known the Order's glory days, and both fear and respect for them was in decline. The Order was increasingly perceived as alien, as was expressed in a popular Prussian saying: 'The Franconian, Swabian and Bavarian kind, do no good to the Prussian land' [41; 102]. The responsibility for the well-being of the whole country, so the Prussian estates felt, now rested with them and no longer with the Order. Encouraged by the Polish king's promise of protection, the Prussian patricians' self-consciousness developed ever more rapidly. By 1437, the phrase 'in defence of our privileges, freedoms and rights' had become a regular formula, evoked during every assembly and in every letter of grievance addressed to the Order. At the same time the legendary antiquity of patrician families, documented in carefully constructed genealogical trees in Danzig, Thorn and Elbing, became part of urban Prussian culture and identity.

Such aspirations helped to forge the solidarity between the noble and urban members of the Prussian League, who promised each other assistance against the Teutonic Order. They demanded an independent law court for the Prussian lands, which was not dominated by the Order but presided over by burghers in the cities and by nobles in the countryside to decide on cases involving their peers. Although the divide-and-rule tactics deployed by successive grand masters enjoyed some success, the alliance rallied during the following decade against all threats of imperial and papal sanctions. The idea that Prussia was an autonomous 'land', free to choose or reject those striving for power over them, took root and forged a strong territorial identity which remained powerful throughout the early modern period [23].

[iv] The Partition of Prussia, 1454–1466

*As it lasts, dear Brother, eat and drink the best,
our Order will not stand time's test.* [362; 255]

The conflict always had an international dimension, both through the support the Prussian representative bodies sought and received from Poland, and the interest of the papacy and the Holy Roman Empire in the fate of the Order. In 1450, a new grand master, the 'hardliner' Ludwig von Erlichshausen, was elected. Under his regime, tensions between Poland and the Order mounted over trade matters, marking Danzig's monopoly position in the trade with Great Poland and Cujavia [46]. Within Poland, leading royalists supported the demands of the Prussian League against the Order and hoped to regain Pomerelia for Poland. To prevent a victory of the Prussian League, the grand master purchased a falsified papal bull which put the organisation under ban. The Prussian League retorted with similar measures, hoping to buy imperial support and preparing an armed rebellion with Polish help. Yet the imperial court refused to listen and decreed the dissolution of the League in November 1453. When rumours spread that the Order was plotting the assassination of their leader, Jan Baysen-Bażyński, in January 1454, the League sent representatives to Poland to negotiate military assistance in case the situation deteriorated further. By February 1454, it had become clear to everyone that war was inevitable.

On 6 March 1454 representatives of the Prussian League decided to agree to the act of incorporation into the kingdom of Poland, which not only held political and economic advantages for the nobles and cities of Prussia, but also for Polish trade in the Baltic. In April, the Prussian estates gathered in Thorn to swear the oath of allegiance in the presence of the bishop of Poznań and the Polish crown chancellor. The Polish declaration of war against the Order was pre-dated to 22 February 1454.

A bloody, 13-year war then ensued, which divided Prussia in two halves: the western provinces and palatinates of Kulm, Marienburg, Pomerelia and the bishopric of Warmia joined the crown of Poland under the name of Royal Prussia (later also called Polish Prussia). The Order managed to retain the eastern half until its secularisation in 1525 under the rule of its last grand master, Albrecht of

Hohenzollern. He followed Martin Luther's advice and dissolved the Order on Prussian soil to restore peace in a situation which had looked increasingly desperate for the Order's decimated troops. In a lavish ceremony on the vast market square in Cracow, Albrecht paid homage to the Polish King Sigismund I 'the Old', who created him the first duke in Prussia, which was now a fief of the Polish crown. It was then that a 'state of estates' (*Ständestaat*) evolved in each part of the divided Prussia, stronger in the western territories, as the Polish crown granted extensive powers of self-government, embodied in the provincial assembly (*Landtag*), or Diet, which gave the cities and nobles equal voices in the political government of their province. In Ducal Prussia, too, the nobles and the capital city of Königsberg formed an influential body of estates that financed and advised their new secular ruler.

Albrecht's oath of feudal submission to the Polish king in 1525, which the nineteenth-century artist Jan Matejko commemorated in a monumental painting known to every Polish schoolchild since its completion in 1882 (see the front cover), became a highly debated political event in German–Polish relations. Polish patriotic historians started to query the wisdom of Poland's sixteenth-century rulers in granting and later extending the succession rights to the whole of the Hohenzollern family in the duchy of Prussia. It was argued that the Polish–Lithuanian army could have easily defeated the Teutonic Order and integrated its territories into Poland once and for all. Guided by their knowledge of the partitions of Poland–Lithuania in the late eighteenth century, such historians condemned the Prussian oath of allegiance of 1525 as a foolish concession which opened the door to German aggression and expansionism [259, 37]. This argument deeply influenced Polish historical attitudes in the modern age, notwithstanding the reality that Poland in 1525 could hardly have been interested in incorporating large stretches of lands devastated by the Teutonic–Polish wars. Sigismund's achievement of securing the duchy as a fief not only avoided further war but also seemed more attractive, as he could intervene directly in the political affairs of the estates when it suited him. German historians also could not agree with Albrecht's arrangement. The feudal oath, if it is mentioned at all by older German literature on the subject, was humiliating to a mentality which considered Germany as the *Kulturträger*, the bearer and promoter of culture and progress in the East.

The Teutonic Legacy

If we discount hindsight, each side had won a victory. Albrecht's mother was Sophia Jagiellonka, the sister of King Sigismund I. Albrecht and Sigismund therefore were cousins. Their alliance was the most viable solution for the last grand master to escape the dilemma posed by a hopelessly weakened Teutonic Order and the absence of any military allies in western Europe. For Poland such an engagement had advantages, as it stipulated that, after Albrecht's death and that of his closest male relatives, Ducal Prussia would fall back to the Polish crown. Above all, in Prussia the Poles had secured an ally who was bound by oath to support them in current and future conflicts with Muscovy, the Ottomans and the Tatars. The price was an imperial and papal ban for Albrecht and a continued critical attitude by the papacy towards Poland. The Polish–Prussian relationship opened up new opportunities for cultural and political exchange across borders and traditions and was perceived as such by contemporaries on both sides. This was particularly true for the estates of Ducal and Royal (Polish) Prussia, who for almost a century to come continued close cooperation in common institutions and participated in the success of the Protestant Reformation, which in Königsberg had found one of its earliest and influential centres in north-east Europe.

2 'State-building'

The rise of Prussia has traditionally been explained in terms of 'state-building'. This approach concentrates on the emergence of central government institutions all focused on the disciplining and policing of society [59]. Recent approaches based on a 'cultural history of politics', however, have queried such all-embracing explanatory models. If the state is a body politic which is continuously negotiated and defined anew through socio-political dialogue and cultural acts, historians have to focus more closely on institutional culture, political practice and human agency [363]. Generations of historians of Prussia, however, applied an influential model of 'top-down' state-building, which failed to address the 'interdependence between discourse and practice', and between the intentions and achievements of those who built the commonweal or 'state' [66, 142].

Several themes have underpinned the state-building approach. The shift of power from corporate organisations of estates (*Stände*) to the ruler as the sole sovereign in the Brandenburg-Prussian territories was presented as a particularly successful example of this phenomenon within European history. The expansion of the military establishment after the Thirty Years War was explained by the concurrent development of Prussia's standing army, which evolved into a quasi-independent apparatus, a 'state within the Prussian state' [366; 121–41]. This perspective drew heavily on Max Weber's idea of the legitimate and rational exercise of power, based on the rule of law and a disciplined, reliable bureaucracy. It is a story of inevitable progress, which historians used to justify the unifying and centralising character of the Prussian military machine [75; 235–45]. If we believe the results of recent historiography on law enforcement and social disciplining, however, Weber's contention that the power of rulership (*Herrschaft*) was an 'opportunity to exact obedience from a target audience', was always just that: an opportunity and a possibility, not a certainty [105]. Can we speak of early modern statehood if its executive power to enforce legislation – whether formulated by the ruler or by the estates – repeatedly failed to function properly? If, as Jürgen Schlumbohm has stressed, one of the main characteristics of early modern statehood was the passing of a large body of laws and ordinances, but the enforcement of very few of them, the whole process of forging a uniform statehood from above, particularly in as heterogeneous a state as Brandenburg-Prussia, becomes even more questionable [108].

These doubts have led to the questioning of the key concept of 'absolutism' since the early 1990s [103, 97, 101, 102, 112]. Apart from some who have found it hard to abandon a long-cherished paradigm [98], a growing consensus suggests that 'absolutism' has lost its explanatory force. The traditional focus on central governmental decrees often ignored local opposition and the inconsistent enforcement of the law by provincial officeholders, thereby underestimating the extent to which absolute government was often circumscribed by political and social reality [89]. Thus we need to look more closely at local circumstances and ask when and how they impacted on the formation of a more integrated political body that could be termed a Brandenburg-Prussian 'state'.

Barbara Stollberg-Rilinger, opposing the tendency to dismiss absolutism altogether, has pointed out the fundamental difference in the understanding by the estates and by the ruler of the principle of representation. The estates, while certainly representing their own interests, also claimed to represent the people's greater common good against the interests of the ruler, particularly if they thought that those interests conflicted with the common good [142]. The prince, however, claimed that through the law of public necessity and utility, he alone had the least partisan knowledge of what was good for the country, thereby justifying his status as the supreme judicial authority [134, 127]. The Hohenzollerns were among the rulers who won this argument. By skilfully instrumentalising natural law teaching they claimed to be the true guardians of the common good, justified to demand complete authority (*summa potestas*) [142; 114].

Thus the transition from composite to unitary state was an intentional political programme, though in political reality it operated at different speeds and with varying success. It was limited by Brandenburg's role as an electoral territory of the Holy Roman Empire. In his political testament, Frederick William, the Great

Elector (r. 1640–88), recommended that his successors take good care of the 'many territories which God's grace bestowed upon us', stressing the inherent danger that the composite nature of his dominions presented [225; 187]. Map 3 demonstrates the security concerns the Elector must have felt when he spoke about these territories as 'members of one head', widely spread across central Europe [75]. If we agree that the early modern Brandenburg-Prussian state was indeed a composite body, or, as John Morrill terms it, a 'dynastic agglomerate', these specific contexts and circumstances must be of concern to students of its history [367]. The rulers' policies of constructing a permanent army and a more centrally coordinated bureaucracy to maximise revenue were strategies of integration to legitimise Hohenzollern ambitions and gain respect from their neighbours. These were priorities for most rulers from the electoral Brandenburg line after 1500, and especially after 1618, when the permanent dynastic union of Brandenburg and Ducal Prussia added a new dimension to the composite nature of Hohenzollern rule.

[i] Instruments of Integration

In the fifteenth century, the Hohenzollerns were upstarts. Other imperial princes, with more illustrious forebears, thought so in 1415, when Frederick, burgrave of Nuremberg (r. 1397–1440), was created Elector of Brandenburg by the Emperor. When Elector Albrecht (r. 1470–86) temporarily united the burgraviate with the Franconian territories of Ansbach, Kulmbach and the Mark Brandenburg, he admitted that his territories had been 'assembled by little more than improvisation' [28; 45]. The history of the Hohenzollern territories before the seventeenth century was not that of a state, but a condominium of territories, sometimes united under one ruler, but more often parcelled out to relatives from various branches of the family.

The history of this family has been written many times. Apart from Prussia, where Albrecht of Brandenburg-Ansbach was appointed grand master of the Teutonic Order in 1511 and became duke in Prussia in 1525 (see Chapter 1), the Hohenzollerns accumulated titles and possessions in Hungary and Silesia, Halberstadt and Magdeburg; in 1514 they temporarily secured the archbishopric of Mainz and its electoral vote. The Franconian branch was particularly active in imperial politics, winning the Emperor's support for its expansion within the Empire and beyond.

Lacking a coherent territory and instruments of statehood during the fifteenth century, the Brandenburg branch tried to make the best of its relatively consolidated north-eastern territories and seeking to establish themselves among the leading imperial princes. Mythical tales of descent from Troy and from senatorial Roman families served to legitimise the electoral position and silence detractors from Wittelsbach Bavaria and other more illustrious dynasties in the struggle for eminence in the imperial hierarchy [28].

Integrating the territories accumulated by the various family branches, however, was not straightforward. The 1473 *Dispositio Achillea*, a family contract, regulated the distribution of the Hohenzollern lands among Albrecht's heirs. It permanently established separate administrations for the Franconian territories of Ansbach and Kulmbach, but stipulated the indivisibility of the Mark Brandenburg. Nevertheless, Elector Joachim I (r. 1499–1535) divided his Brandenburg territories between his first-born, Joachim II (r. 1535–71), and his second-born, John (of Küstrin, r. 1535–71), who received the Neumark. The parts were only reunited after 1571.

After 1500, contemporary references to the 'house of Brandenburg' denoted a sense of union which did not exist in political reality [28; 51–3]. That the dynasty was well aware that it alone linked its disparate territorial holdings is reflected in the Gera contract of 1598 (confirmed in 1603), guaranteeing the unity of all Hohenzollern territories in the Empire under the electoral line of Brandenburg, after the Franconian margrave George Frederick of Ansbach (r. 1543–1603) died without leaving an heir. It failed, however, to prevent the younger sons of Elector John George of Brandenburg (r. 1571–98), the heirs to Ansbach and Kulmbach, founding their own branches. Their descendants ruled there until 1791, when the last, childless margrave Charles Alexander sold his territories to the electoral line [138] (see Appendix 1).

Franconia nevertheless remained a major source of support for Brandenburg and – after 1525 – for Ducal Prussia. Financial and administrative personnel, troops and money were transferred from the south-western imperial lands to the north-east, though the Ansbach court still took precedence over Berlin well into the sixteenth century. Hohenzollern policies resemble the family politics of late medieval patrimonial rulers. As in other parts of the fifteenth-century Empire, institutions were established to give a structure to territorial statehood. These developments do not need to be couched in teleological language, particularly as they were far from linear and were the joint achievement of the dynasty and its local elites. The administrative and political instruments which developed between the sixteenth and early eighteenth centuries were varied and numerous. Appendix 2 will help to give a better idea of some of their functions, chronology and location.

Judicial reform was one of the earliest measures intended to strengthen the ruler's role, but it was also one of the areas which reflected most persistently the composite character of the Hohenzollern lands. Jurisdiction in the Hohenzollerns' imperial territories was not isolated from the development of law elsewhere in the Empire. Replacing medieval community-based law courts, the electors followed the imperial example of using Roman law to centralise legal structures. Under the influence of Emperor Charles V's Codex Carolina of 1532, Hohenzollern princes began claiming greater powers over criminal cases, while civil law remained under the jurisdiction of the estates and towns. From 1516, starting with electoral Brandenburg, each province received new high courts (*Kammergerichte*), though the prince claimed the right to confirm their decisions as the highest, supra-territorial judge. After the Reformation, ecclesiastical matters were decided by central consistorial courts, while most cases connected with the administration of the state domains continued to be dealt with in castle and district courts. After 1604, the coordination of these courts fell to the newly-founded Brandenburg Privy Council, which – later than in most other comparable German territories – assumed new, central jurisdictional and policy-making competences [77, 81]. If this was the first step towards 'creating a state administration' [85; 26], it failed, as its remit was restricted to the coordination of Brandenburg policy alone, and attempts to extend the Privy Council's jurisdiction to all Hohenzollern territories were abandoned. After 1550, there was no clear, linear tendency towards centralisation, as the estates strengthened their influence in return for liquidating the rulers' growing debts, maintaining their control over provincial jurisdiction, at least in civil matters. Thus until the mid-seventeenth century, most administrative innovations remained restricted to the provincial level and built on local traditions. Despite a long historiographical tradition stressing this dualism of interest between ruler and estates, the electors could ill afford to ignore the

'State-building'

estates' functions of giving credit and providing defence. This was a relationship built on mutual trust. The confirmation of privileges by the ruler acknowledged that he could not integrate and defend his composite state without the estates' assistance (see Chapter 3).

Cooperation functioned least smoothly in newly-acquired territories and lands peripheral to Brandenburg's electoral core. In Ducal Prussia Frederick William faced strong resistance to the introduction of a new High Tribunal (*Obertribunal*) in 1660/1, after securing sovereignty over the duchy three years earlier. Freed of Polish overlordship, the elector sought to strengthen his power over the province. The Prussian nobles continued in vain to claim the right of appeal to the Polish king and to be judged only by their peers, after the model of the elected noble tribunals in Poland.

In 1703, the estates in most Imperial Hohenzollern territories also lost their right of appeal to the Emperor's courts. Leopold I, who needed Brandenburg-Prussia's military and diplomatic support, granted the newly crowned Prussian king Frederick I the privilege of no appeal for matters involving less than 2500 thalers. Frederick seized this opportunity to create a more uniform justice system. He immediately introduced a highest appeal court, except for electoral Brandenburg, where the *Kammergericht* already fulfilled this function. The limited nature of this privilege, however, meant that it did not completely separate Brandenburg from the Empire in jurisdictional matters. This imperial context continued to limit 'absolute rule' until Frederick II finally removed his subjects' right of appeal to the Emperor between 1742 and 1750 (see Chapter 6).

Central taxation is the other grand theme usually associated with 'state-building'. The devastating consequences of the Thirty Years War brought home to the Hohenzollerns how woefully inadequate their military and financial preparations had been. In 1626, Swedish troops reached Prussia and collected heavy contributions from the local population, who for two decades remained under almost permanent foreign occupation. Instead of liberating his territories from military burdens when the enemy vacated the land, Frederick William, who succeeded his father George William in 1640, continued collecting the contribution in peacetime. It was George William's Catholic minister, count Adam von Schwarzenberg, who first developed this policy, using the Brandenburg War Council to reduce the power of the estates and the role of the Privy Council between 1630 and 1641. He appointed war commissars on the Swedish model, with a similar role to *intendants aux armées* in France [61, 71, 306]. They were coordinated by a military office which controlled the distribution of money for the maintenance of troops. Regular contributions replaced the irregular feudal levy, dependent on the consent of the estates, which had proved wholly inadequate after 1620. Centrally-appointed war commissars replaced officials chosen by the provincial estates. In Brandenburg Frederick William thus took the first step towards administrative and fiscal centralisation for all territories under Hohenzollern rule by installing the General War Commissariat in 1660.

The introduction after 1667 of the excise (*Akzise*), a tax levied on consumption, was particularly distasteful to the estates. Substantial noble resistance ensured that the excise was an exclusively urban tax, collected in Brandenburg from 1667, in Prussia from 1680, in Pomerania from 1682 and in Magdeburg from 1688. The quarrel between nobles and towns over the excise divided the opposition, weakened the estates and disadvantaged the urban economy.

Yet the Elector could not and did not ride roughshod over all provincial variations. Following the model of Ducal Prussia, where a separate Prussian war chancery was founded in 1656 during the Second Northern War (see Chapter 5), other Hohenzollern territories also received war chambers, which acquired their own jurisdiction, often taking into account local traditions. Aware of the composite character of his territories, Elector Frederick William reinforced his influence within each part through provincial offices, called *Amtskammern*, as a counterweight to territorial government councils: Electoral Brandenburg (1652), Cleves-Mark (1653), Eastern Pomerania (1654), Ducal Prussia (1661) and Magdeburg (1680) (see Appendix 2). Provincial governments were staffed from local elites whose willingness to cooperate with the Elector's policies varied (see Chapter 3). Where he faced more resistance, as in Cleves and Ducal Prussia, the Elector systematically promoted foreigners to high positions. Men like Adam von Schwarzenberg or Georg von Waldeck after 1651, who had no connections with the native nobility, had to rely on the Elector for advancement [87]. The idea was not new: Duke Albrecht had done the same in Prussia in the 1560s, appointing a host of Franconian advisers and evoking vociferous protests from members of the estates, whose lucrative career opportunities were thereby blocked. The drive for integration increasingly clashed with the interests of local elites.

'State-building'

Institutions which had grown up in a specific territorial context and were controlled by the estates did not disappear overnight, but some of them lost considerable influence (see Chapter 3). The new acquisition of territories such as Pomerania, Magdeburg and Minden after 1648 provided a welcome opportunity for the Hohenzollerns to make the transition to a more centrally-controlled style of government. The governors and administrations introduced in these territories came armed with new tax systems, a relocation of offices and the appointment of foreigners. The Table of Offices (Appendix 2), however, shows that relatively few new institutions functioned at supra-territorial level before the eighteenth century. Most were introduced and adapted to provincial needs and conditions.

The early eighteenth century brought further change to the composite nature of the Hohenzollern territories. Several powerful new institutions elevated the importance of the capital Berlin under Frederick III/I (1689–1713). After he secured royal status in 1701 (see Chapter 4), he abolished the remaining provincial-level estate assemblies. He created the Brandenburg *Hofkammer* in 1689 as a political forum which, after 1713, turned into the General Finance Directory, the highest finance office for all Hohenzollern territories. Subject to the *Hofkammer*, the provincial *Amtskammern* now ruled over the domains, the religious consistories and the war commissariats, which in turn administered excise collection, custom tolls, trades and crafts, and other financial matters, including tax negotiations with the estates (see Appendix 2).

Under Frederick William I (r. 1713–40), who prioritised the army and a more efficient financial administration over investment in a representative Baroque court, the distance between the monarch amidst his circle of advisers and the population at large increased considerably. This certainly contributed to his image as the most 'absolute' of all Hohenzollern monarchs, ruling through a fierce personal regime. The foundation in 1728 of a Department of Foreign and Public Affairs, a small, albeit institutionalised and qualified group of advisers around the king, deprived the old privy council of its last vital function (see Chapter 4).

By uniting the War Commissariat and the General Finance Directory in 1722–3, Frederick William created an institution with the cumbersome name of *General-Ober-Finanz-Kriegs-und-Domänen-Direktorium* (in short, General Directory), located in the castle in Berlin. The internal structure of this office, with its nine war and domain chambers, reflected the territorial divisions of the composite state, but it also indicated that they were now all led from the main residence, which the king, despite his parsimony, continued to build and improve.

Only at a first glance, however, is this a narrative of irresistible centralisation and 'state-building'. Many central ordinances had little effect, having been reissued time and time again and adapted to provincial conditions; several measures could only be partly implemented. Thus plans to rotate officials throughout the provinces every three years were decisively rejected by the territorial estates, governors and *Amtskammern*. Networks of patronage and collusion between local elites and royal bureaucrats continued to grow, and were sometimes consciously exploited by the monarch himself to prevent provincial interests rejecting central policies. The Great Elector issued decrees banning the native nobility entering foreign service on twelve occasions between 1654 and 1687, yet service abroad, particularly from Hohenzollern border territories, continued well into the eighteenth century [75; 243]. Tax expected and tax collected rarely coincided, contributing to the Hohenzollern chamber's need for more income amidst chronic complaints about their provincial governments' unreliability. More importantly, however, the accommodation of local elites in central offices and the increasingly important military apparatus contributed to the easing of tensions and strengthened cooperation between local territorial powers and central authority. The recruitment of councillors from among the local elites signalled the construction of a hierarchy of officials, whose tasks ultimately led them from collecting taxes in the districts to holding offices in the growing central bureaucracy.

[ii] The Military as an Instrument of State-building

After the monopoly over taxation and jurisdiction, the military was one of the most effective instruments by which disparate territories and elites might be united behind one cause. By the eighteenth century, Prussian military success had built a legitimacy which was vital in cementing a unity of purpose at a political and psychological level. This development was far from predictable during the sixteenth and seventeenth centuries, when recruits to the armies of the Elector/Duke were rarely motivated by support for the person of the ruler or by patriotic sentiments.

'State-building'

There is no doubt that Prussia gained its reputation and standing among Europe's powers by expanding its army and by its successful participation in what Michael Roberts first termed the 'military revolution'. Yet this traditional picture needs some qualification. If we understand the military revolution not merely as a revolution of military techniques and organisation, but, as Roberts argued, the social and political revolution that heralded the 'fiscal-military state', Brandenburg-Prussia's version of this revolution built on its role as an auxiliary power which was a useful ally for larger players in Europe [298, 305]. Moreover, the Empire's constitutional division into ten Circles (*Kreise*), which were responsible for organising imperial defence, provided limitations but also opportunities for princes to build their territorial armies [309; 17–22]. Each Circle allocated military burdens for the defence of the Empire collecting contributions in the form of money and men. From 1681, cash allocations could free territories from sending actual troops, while states with extended military structures in place benefited from this arrangement by fielding their armies in return for payments. Brandenburg-Prussia was one of the beneficiaries.

One of the major problems a territorial army faced was recruitment. During the Thirty Years War, the search for suitable recruits was driven by a complex system of contractors, military entrepreneurs and trading agents who sought financial benefit. Men who voluntarily joined the army were either adventurous, poor and seeking out a secure position, or escaping intolerable personal conditions, and in some cases a criminal past [366; 121–41]. Brandenburg-Prussian legislation had tried to regulate recruitment to lessen the impact on local economies. Those who paid taxes and worked in respected professions were in theory unwelcome as soldiers, as they contributed to society in other useful ways. Although coercion was officially banned, forced recruitment was still widespread, as men were plied with alcohol and threatened with violence. Bureaucrats in the local civil offices (*Ämter*) faced a difficult choice between helping the recruitment effort and maintaining the labour force of a fragile economy. Excesses diminished somewhat when Frederick William dissolved the War Council in 1641 and reinstated the Privy Council to its former influence in a move aimed at winning the estates' good will and support for his policies [60].

Through a policy of collecting subsidies and the clever exploitation of favourable political constellations following the Thirty Years War,

Elector Frederick William was the first to reap the benefits. Yet the Elector's troops in the Second Northern War in Poland did not yet constitute anything resembling a standing army (see Chapter 5). Owing to the administrative and territorial separation of the central Privy Council from the local resources that paid for and supplied the army with men, the beginnings of the Prussian standing army rested on vulnerable foundations. Hybrid forms of army expansion, such as voluntary recruitment, the remnants of the noble levy, and the beginnings of a regular draft of subjects coexisted well into the early decades of the eighteenth century [309, 310]. In 1679, the Brandenburg forces were reduced from 45,000 to 25,000, but many of those demobilised were new recruits, who were constantly moved around, so that no firm identification either with the ruler or the 'state' developed. In contrast to the Swedish armies, Brandenburg still relied mostly on mercenaries and continued to accept subsidies for its auxiliary role on the Emperor's side in the War of the Spanish Succession after 1701. Frederick I rented out 8000 troops in return for 150,000 florins and the prize of the royal crown (see Chapter 4).

In the pursuit of greater glory and the expansion of his army, Frederick even revived the Prussian noble levy, a land militia raised by native noblemen from the domains and urban guards, who filled the place of the regular army when it fought abroad. From a ruler's perspective the militia's main drawback was its defensive agenda and its dependence on the estates, whose influence Frederick wanted to diminish politically, but who persisted in determining the size and nature of this force reflecting local resources. The flexible use of troops, such as granting leave of absence to soldiers needed for harvesting, was also common to militia systems in other territories of the Holy Roman Empire [311; 16].

Subsidies helped sustain the army well into the eighteenth century: even Frederick II accepted them, despite the criticism he levelled at his predecessors for doing the same. Remnants from the past endured for longer than traditional historiography has admitted, and the outcome of the 'military revolution' in Brandenburg-Prussia was mixed. It certainly cannot be presented simply as the victory of the central state over local decision-making, as Johann Kunisch did in stating that 'the conflict over the military finally separated monarchic authority and the estates' [104; 86]. It is true that the estates had lost their effective control over the army as creditors when they could not stop the financial and military breakdown of their territories during the Thirty Years War. After 1648, they increasingly lost control over whether money and troops were raised, but they could still influence how they were raised, as practice varied from territory to territory.

Throughout the 1720s, Frederick William I tried to solve a problem which confronted all contemporary European powers: how to secure the supply of manpower necessary to sustain a standing army without hurting the economy that supported it. His solution was the Kanton system, introduced in 1733. Based on an annual quota, operated by district officials familiar with local conditions, the male population was enrolled in lists, from which the army was supplemented every year. Enlisted men had to undergo regular training but were only called to active duty when required. In peacetime they worked in their civilian jobs for ten months of the year while 'furloughed' (on leave) from military duty, although they and their families remained under military jurisdiction and had to report regularly. Following Otto Hintze, Otto Büsch blamed the Kanton system for the 'social militarization' of Prussian society, to which nobles seemed to be particularly receptive, since they allegedly combined two functions: that of officers over the men under their command, and that of landowners and feudal lords over their serfs. Thus, according to Büsch, Prussian subjects suffered under the double authority of the officer-landlord who reinforced the close relationship between political and military power [296]. While older historiography usually presented the Kanton system as a precursor to the general draft in terms of patriotic duty, Büsch's claims concerning the politicisation of the recruitment system suggest that the Kanton system was exceptional in laying the foundations for Prussia's future authoritarianism and militarism.

As Peter Wilson has shown, however, officers usually did not recruit their own serfs; many nobles who joined the officer corps did not even own landed estates [311; 24]. For many poorer peasants service in the army meant a degree of emancipation both from their village and from their landlord. A wide range of tasks eroded the influence which landlords possessed over the landed population in their role as company commanders. Yet if local magistrates and village communities were granted a role in the administration of the Kanton system that suited their need to control local society, this was not a Prussian peculiarity, but was a feature of the seventeenth-century Swedish military reforms and was widely adopted by other eighteenth-century states. Wilson's critique of Büsch has been echoed by Jürgen Kloosterhuis and, more recently, by Martin Winter. While Kloosterhuis stresses the need to examine strategies of popular resistance in Prussian Westphalia [300; 177–90], where only 6 per cent of the population were enlisted, Winter focuses on more neglected aspects of the system, such as its impact on urban society and economy [312]. They both deny the direct link that Büsch was so keen to establish between the system of landed economy (*Gutsherrschaft*) (see Chapter 3) and the success of the Kanton system. Considering the large – albeit greatly varying – number of exemptions from Kanton service across the Brandenburg-Prussian provinces, there was no simple connection between rural power structures and the development of the army: some of the western provinces such as East Frisia (after 1744) remained exempt from the Kanton system; in Silesia in 1743–4 only just under 1500 men were enrolled out of a population of 1.2 million, whereas in Ansbach and Bayreuth, the old Hohenzollern heartlands in Franconia, almost a quarter of males had to join the army [311; 19]. What the Prussian monarchy did achieve, however, was a 'unique exploitation of the corporate structures of noble society for the organisation of the army', particularly the lower nobility, who gained new career perspectives and benefited from the protection of its rural labour force [182].

In 1717 Frederick William tackled the problem of the noble levy by declaring the allodification of all fiefs: losing their feudal status, landed estates could now be freely bought and sold. In return their owners had to pay a regular military contribution of 50 thalers to support the cavalry. The nobility in Brandenburg swiftly agreed to these changes. The von Kleists embraced the new legislation as it strengthened their property rights against the claims of various kin groups; this security encouraged them to invest more generously in the long term and allowed consolidation of landownership in one branch of the family [184; 305]. There is also evidence that as a result of allodification, rural subjects and nobility alike adopted the habit of mutually leasing estates, commercialising agrarian activities further and thus overcoming corporate and social status barriers [195; 404–33].

Other provincial nobilities resisted, not least because of widely differing feudal regulations in the Hohenzollern provinces, and because the newly-standardised contribution raised taxation levels in some provinces more than in others [80]. The scheme met powerful opposition in Pomerania, which provides a good case study for the integrative force of the Brandenburg-Prussian army, as it was a theatre of operations during the Thirty Years War and again in the 1650s and 1670s. As in Magdeburg, which the Hohenzollerns could only incorporate in 1680, noble resistance in Pomerania focused on the changing relationship of the vassal to his lord from one of loyalty and mutual assistance towards one of 'mere obedience and subjection'. The king failed to convince the Pomeranian nobles of the many advantages of allodification, such as the right to dispose of their estates at will. The Pomeranian nobles were particularly incensed that their less densely populated province had to send more horses per head of population than other Hohenzollern dominions [80; 50–1]. Piqued by gibes from their Polish neighbours that they had become mere peasants, the provincial estates even turned, in vain, to Poland for help. Allodification in Pomerania was not formally agreed until 1786, although military taxation had been in force since 1717, ignoring the tax-free status which the nobility of most territories enjoyed in the Holy Roman Empire.

Integration policies in Pomerania were boycotted on other levels. A training academy founded in 1655 for young nobles in Kolberg soon moved to Berlin owing to a lack of interest, largely due to its Calvinist orientation, to which Lutheran Pomeranian noble society reacted with as much hostility as to the foreign Calvinist elites, usually Huguenots, who in the 1680s began to fill Pomeranian offices. Instead, young Pomeranian nobles continued to seek their fortune in cadet schools abroad and in the foreign armies of Denmark, Poland, Sweden, Saxony and the Empire, until Frederick William I closed the borders, imposing draconian punishment for what he labelled 'desertion' [200; 107–9]. Military academies within their reach were meant to replace the training which noble officers traditionally experienced through service assignments on foreign battlefields [301; 85–8]

In the long term, however, the army was accepted as a career ladder even in Pomerania. Preference given to nobles in the officer corps, and Frederick William I's personal favours for his 'loyal Pomeranians' appealed to poorer nobles, who experienced upward social mobility. As a result of such a carrot-and-stick policy, Pomeranians began to fill the lower officer ranks, which were most exposed to the dangers of warfare. The Seven Years War hit the

Pomeranian noble elite hard and affected their presence in the army for half a century to come. Smaller landowners disappeared, landownership became concentrated in the hands of a reduced elite, which led many to fill provincial administrative offices, where they excelled as enlightened bureaucrats in the later eighteenth century.

[iii]   Territorial Integration – Confessional Division?

Early modern Brandenburg-Prussia is usually thought of as a united 'Protestant' power. But resistance by its composite parts against confessional integration did not only come from the numerous Catholics of the territories annexed during the eighteenth century (Silesia, western Poland); Protestantism was also sharply divided between a Lutheran and a Reformed (Calvinist) variant. The great proponent of natural law, Justus Lipsius (1547–1606), whose ideas Elector Frederick William absorbed during his studies in Leiden, was adamant that a state needed to preserve confessional unity in order to maintain stability. For a Calvinist ruling house, which aimed to displace Lutheran Saxony as leader of the Empire's Protestants, the hostility of its majority Lutheran population was an existential issue and a significant obstacle to state-building.

The process by which churches and secular rulers alike sought to define religious denominations along doctrinal lines by controlling the clergy and disciplining the population has been termed 'confessionalisation', first by Ernst Walter Zeeden, but more consequentially by Heinz Schilling and Wolfgang Reinhard [172, 169]. While first perceived as a top-down process based on the princes' right to reform their territorial churches (*ius reformandi*) granted in the 1555 peace of Augsburg, recent research has established how social, political and ecclesiastical structures interacted to polarise the emerging confessional groups.

After the 1525 secularisation of the Teutonic Order, Albrecht was the first prince – albeit outside the Empire – to embrace and implement Lutheran ideas. Luther's protests against the Catholic Church had in part been inspired by his hostility to the indulgences sold in the name of Albrecht, cardinal and prince bishop of Mainz. The cardinal was a relative of Albrecht of Prussia, a brother of Elector Joachim I, and one of the main instigators of the 1521 Edict of Worms that placed Luther and his followers under imperial ban. Family relations

'State-building'

between the Ansbach Franconian and the Brandenburg lines, therefore, were poor [166]. While Albrecht invited Lutheran theologians to his newly-founded duchy, Joachim I sought to stop the Reformation from crossing into his electorate. Not only did he side firmly with the Emperor, but he also joined other Catholic princes in rejecting the 1530 Lutheran Augsburg Confession and suppressed the evangelical movement in his cities. Neither confessional unity nor territorial consolidation seemed achievable for the Hohenzollerns. Although both Joachim I's sons became Protestants, after the division of Brandenburg in 1535 into the Neumark under John of Küstrin, and the Electoral Mark under Joachim II, John turned out to be the more radical follower of the Reformation when in 1538 he joined the anti-Catholic Schmalkaldic League. His brother, partly restrained by the influence of his Catholic Polish wife, partly due to his own conciliatory approach to both confessions and his cautious policies towards the Emperor, only sanctioned Lutheran reforms in 1539, under pressure from his estates. He made sure that the 1540 Brandenburg Church Ordinance was the most moderate of all Lutheran ecclesiastical statutes in the Empire [166].

Joachim II was more radical when he dissolved the monasteries and claimed church property for the relief of his indebted treasury [176]. While John of Küstrin and Albrecht of Prussia rejected the 1548 Augsburg *Interim*, which restored several core Catholic teachings, the conservative Lutheran theologian Johann Agricola from Brandenburg helped draft it. Elector John George adopted it in 1571, consolidating what became known as Gnesio-Lutheranism, which imposed a strictly Lutheran line on preaching and teaching, rejecting Philipp Melanchthon's irenicism, and committing the Brandenburg church to the conservative Wittenberg *Formula Concordiae* of 1577.

Cracks appeared in Lutheran unity under Joachim Frederick (r. 1598–1608), who after 32 years as administrator of Magdeburg succeeded his father as Elector in 1598. Inviting foreign councillors, he managed to split the recently-created Privy Council into traditionalists and newcomers, some of whom unashamedly sympathised with Calvinism. His choice of Anna of Prussia, heir to the duchy of Cleves, to marry his son John Sigismund (r. 1608–19), was as shrewd as his contacts with Reformed princes, such as the Elector Palatine [167]. Hohenzollern awareness of the threat from a rejuvenated, post-Tridentine Catholicism was as much a motive as dynastic interest.

Hintze exaggerated the impact that John Sigismund's 1613 conversion to Calvinism had on Prussia's rise to great power status, but the event was certainly significant, albeit not a resounding success for top-down confessionalisation [160; 71]. The 1614 church ordinance, the *Confessio Sigismundi*, provoked fierce public protests against this Second (Calvinist) Reformation from above. Lutheran opposition ensured that Calvinism remained restricted to the prince's immediate entourage: the electoral and ducal courts, the Privy Council, and a small circle of Reformed preachers, all heavily reliant on princely favour. This meant, however, that they not only shared the prince's confessional beliefs but also his political ambitions. Such loyalty bound religion and politics inseparably together [166; 109].

Calvinist support for a more centralist, absolute style of government seems odd in the context of French or Dutch Calvinism, which fought against strong monarchy and dabbled in the monarchomach theories that legitimised regicide as a means of resistance to tyranny. Calvinism in Brandenburg was neither radical, nor republican, nor monarchomach. In its Lutheran as well as its Calvinist forms, the Reformation in Brandenburg-Prussia remained a princely Reformation, but also demonstrated the limits of religious power politics and confessionalisation from above. The myth that Calvinism was by nature more 'democratic' and consensual, mainly due to its presbyterian structures, certainly does not apply to Brandenburg-Prussia, where no presbyterianism developed as the ruler assumed the episcopal role.

The relationship between state-building and confessional development in Brandenburg and Prussia is open to debate: to what extent did pragmatism and utility dictate the confessional course of the Hohenzollern dynasty, even if we allow for the sincere religiosity of its rulers? And to what extent, if at all, did religion work for or against the integration of diverse territories? Nineteenth-century Prussian historians such as Ranke and Droysen linked Prussian 'Protestantism' with an emerging Prusso-German nationalism, which left no space for alternative narratives. Anti-Calvinist protests by the Lutheran establishment, linked to the estates' resistance to centralising measures, were either ignored or discussed in a negative light. Instead, the Hohenzollerns earned praise for their policy of toleration [160, 158, 3]. Yet toleration was not the expression of a tolerant mindset, but a practical tool, 'judged by its utility for the state' [146; 269]. It was political necessity that forced John Sigismund in his 1614 religious ordinance to confirm that 'his Electoral Highness will not publicly or secretly force any of his subjects against their will to accept this confession' [26; 353–6].

This promise was not believed by many Lutherans. They insisted on assurances: every new tax had to be bought with concessions and pledges not to violate the estates' religious privileges or their presentation rights. The Elector had to promise that he would not appoint Calvinist preachers where he owned the right of presentation himself [166; 210]. The Ducal Prussian Lutherans were particularly suspicious of Brandenburg authorities – more so, it seems, than they were of the Polish king, who in 1613–16 had a Catholic church built in, and financed by, the city of Königsberg [205; 61]. King Władysław IV repaid the city by protecting it against George William's tax demands in 1632–5. The duke's dependence on his Polish overlord still provided the Prussian estates with a powerful weapon. More than once they secured from Warsaw guarantees for their Lutheran religion, while accusing the Calvinists of plotting revolt against their Polish suzerain [261]. In this triangle between Prussia, Poland and Brandenburg, the Prussian estates retained autonomies – both religious and political – which no other territorial estates enjoyed under Hohenzollern rule, and which most effectively prevented the spread of Calvinism in Ducal Prussia.

Some initiatives for confessional union between the Reformed and the Lutheran churches were not imposed from above, but came from below. At the height of the Catholic threat during the Thirty Years War, Calvinists and Lutherans cooperated and even considered common theological ground, as in the Leipzig Colloquy of 1631. The 1645 Colloquy of Thorn, an initiative of Władysław IV of Poland, failed, not least due to the Lutherans' strict adherence to the Wittenberg line, which made any contacts between conciliatory Lutherans and Calvinists fruitless [165].

The promotion of Reformed irenicism became Brandenburg's imperfect vehicle for confessional brokerage between the Calvinist dynasty and the Lutheran population. The Lutheran consistory, closely supportive of the strictly Lutheran line of the 1577 *Formula Concordiae*, fought an ineffective new (Reformed) church council, while Reformed schools were boycotted and destroyed in the war, before being re-established under Elector Frederick William in the 1650s [216; 121–48]. The Reformed university in Frankfurt/Oder similarly failed to become the magnet for Reformed education the electors wished it to be. The failure of Frederick, Elector Palatine, in his role as king of Bohemia, and the victory of the Catholic forces at the battle of the White Mountain in 1620 further discredited political Calvinism in Brandenburg and contributed to the rise of Schwarzenberg's pro-Habsburg policies under Elector George William. The Reformed church in the Hohenzollern territories seemed all but dead.

The Peace of Westphalia changed much. With Calvinism established as an official confession alongside Lutheranism, and with the estates economically weakened by the war, Frederick William was able to help the Reformed church to gain the upper hand. He did so increasingly with the support of the French Huguenots, who entered the country in large numbers even before the revocation of the Edict of Nantes in 1685. He also mustered support from the Dutch and from Cleves, who fostered Reformed networks in all Hohenzollern territories. What Bodo Nischan saw too optimistically as cooperation between an irenic church leadership and the elector's policies of toleration, remained predominantly restricted to the ruler's sphere, in a phenomenon described by Volker Press as 'court Calvinism' [168]. After 1648 government institutions demonstrated a new quality of rulership which aimed at undermining the deeply-rooted Lutheran culture of Brandenburg- Prussia. In the county of Mark, for example, Frederick William openly favoured Calvinism in a province where confessional division had traditionally been managed peacefully in local communities, outside the ruler's sphere of influence. The ruler's partisan attitude introduced sharp conflicts in everyday life, mainly focused on church properties and local privileges [145; 218–19].

The exclusion of the estates from confessional matters was a particular bone of contention. When the Elector presented them with a new Lutheran consistorial statute, he commented that 'such ordinances were only in the territorial ruler's exclusive power, as he alone possessed all episcopal rights' [160; 77]. When he forced foreign Calvinists into high offices in Ducal Prussia, in 1663, he violated both political and religious guarantees. The 1685 Potsdam Edict, which allowed French Calvinists to settle in Brandenburg, was hardly an act of toleration, as it suited the dynasty to attract co-religionists whose services it could muster against Lutheran opposition.

'State-building'

The influx of tens of thousands of Huguenots to the court and into the cities alienated the noble and urban elites even further. The frequently hostile reception by the local Lutheran population forged a strong group identity among the Huguenots which delayed their assimilation, but also ensured they were the ruler's most faithful servants. The Elector gave them tax breaks, helped with their settlement, preferred them for offices and supported their crafts, churches, schools and separate law courts, which they retained until 1806 [156; 107–28]. Their language and origin also boosted their image as representatives of a civilised avant-garde among the European elites who used French as the new *lingua franca* of scholarship, diplomacy and courtly life [257; 210–11].

The Huguenots repaid their patron with unmitigated hero-worship. They were rewarded by a privileged status in the cities and at court, where they built close-knit family networks, occasionally branching out into intermarriage with the local aristocracy. Many Huguenots embraced 'Prussiandom' more vigorously than provincial elites who continued to resist integration by maintaining their Pomeranian, Frisian, Silesian or Rhenish identities [156; 122–3]. Due to their mainly urban backgrounds, the Prussian Huguenots developed their highly specialised manufacturing and mercantile talents. The eighteenth-century courtier and adventurer Karl Ludwig von Pöllnitz, in his characteristically exaggerated style, praised them as inventors of Prussia's manufactures: 'They gave us the first idea of trade which we did not know beforehand. They founded Berlin's police, part of the city's paved streets, introduced abundance and well-being, and made this city one of the most beautiful in Europe ... they softened our rough habits and elevated us to the status of an enlightened nation' [156; 147]. The Huguenots lacked, however, the confidence to emancipate themselves from their dependence on the monarchy. This is important when considering that of almost 20,000 Huguenot immigrants in Brandenburg-Prussia, 40 per cent settled in the Berlin area and constituted a fifth of the overall urban population of the capital city towards the end of the eighteenth century [156; 67–79]. Their cultural and technical influence was significant for Prussia's modernisation, yet their political role was conservative. Historians have spoken of a '*Ersatz*-citizenry' that had little understanding for traditions of self-government and native concerns about forced recruitment and the destruction of communal autonomy during the eighteenth century [161].

The Reformed church functioned as an integrative tool for all those willing to follow the Elector's lead. The Lutheran estates' most hated target was the Calvinist Prussian Dohna family, whose support for the Hohenzollerns was rewarded at the court. Abraham von Dohna helped negotiate the Brandenburg succession in Ducal Prussia with the Polish king Sigismund III, and made no secret of his hostility towards the Lutheran estates which, he believed, acted as agents of the Polish counter-Reformation [139, 149]. He also played a key role on the predominantly Calvinist governmental council (*Oberrat*) and through contacts to influential Calvinist families, particularly in Poland-Lithuania, who sought international support against re-catholicisation in their own country [174; 103–20].

Following Hintze and Gerhard Oestreich, historians have argued that Calvinism injected a dynamism which made the Brandenburg-Prussian model a success unparalleled in the Empire and beyond. In this sense, Philip S. Gorski's thesis that its rise to power cannot be understood without regard to its religious situation, deserves consideration [155; 80]. The association of Calvinism with modernisation works only within an explanatory model focused on the role of the ruler and top-down state-building. Integration, centralisation and disciplining by the state, however, remained less than complete. This approach also ignores the importance of regional forces, the resistance of the estates, the church and the wider population. It omits the larger European context and the limitations which all of these factors imposed on Prussian development before the nineteenth century.

3 Estate Society and Life in the Rural Economy

[i] Social Structures and Civil Society

The rural economy in Brandenburg-Prussia has not had a good press. As the militarised Prussian Junker class was widely blamed for two world wars, most post-war English-language works maintained a negative attitude towards it. German historians mostly followed Hintze, whose works focused on a nobility which accepted their prince's absolute sovereignty in return for their new roles as bureaucrats and army officers [125, 39]. Büsch presented an influential image of a jingoist East-Elbian noble class that became the negative blueprint by which Germany's supposedly undemocratic traditions could be historically explained [296]. Studies by Carsten and Hans Rosenberg perpetuated the vision of the Prussian nobility as a serf-owning, bureaucratised caste worshipping an authoritarian state, which deviated substantially from 'normal' European and 'Western' development [11, 179]. In the late 1980s, Robert M. Berdahl summarised this attitude in his emphasis on the Junkers' conservative patriarchal ideology which apparently resisted both market forces and public-spirited reforms [178].

If state-building was indeed an instrument of integration which turned the 'personal union' between the Hohenzollern territories into a 'real union', as Wolfgang Neugebauer has stressed, it must have also embraced the estates in the diverse territories under Hohenzollern rule [9; 48]. Do we know what their political programmes were? To what extent did they oppose or cooperate with state-building processes? Monika Wienfort's comment, that regional nobilities only had their own, selfish interest in mind, misses the point [17; 24]: why should the newly-annexed territorial estates of

Cleves have wished to provide taxes to meet commitments in the Altmark, hundreds of miles away? Why indeed should the worthy people of Prussia have been interested in the 'state', when there was none but the ruler's will which openly sought to diminish the political liberties they had accumulated over centuries?

This apparent dualism between ruler and estates lies at the heart of a long and fruitful historiographical tradition. Gerhard Oestreich and Marc Raeff have analysed the relationship between the 'police state' and 'social disciplining' [86, 89, 107; 205–27], while older German liberal historians from Otto von Gierke onwards emphasised corporate, communal and republican traditions which in turn fertilised research on urban and noble communities, by Dietrich Gerhard, Peter Blickle, and Koenigsberger among others [123, 122, 147, 128, 119]. Since the 1980s historians, instead of approaching Brandenburg-Prussian history on the traditional assumption of dichotomy between the prince and the estates, have stressed the 'non-absolute in absolutism' and the 'permanence of the estates' and their institutions, even after the formal exclusion of the estate assemblies from political decision-making [111, 91, 143, 130, 59]. There is scope, however, to go further by integrating the estates into the analysis of the state as a proactive force, not as an obstacle to princely state-building.

The growing recognition of Brandenburg-Prussia's mixed heritage of western and east-central European political cultures and the clash of their different values, conventions and political practices has complicated the historical debate but added an important new dimension to it. For example, it is significant that state-building approaches which consider the integration of the composite body of Brandenburg-Prussia from the top down, rarely if ever mention the concept of citizenship [120]. Yet the Ducal Prussian estates – with an eye on their fellow noblemen across the border in Polish Prussia – regularly argued that they were part of civil society, embracing what Klaus Zernack has called the 'East-Central European *libertas*-culture', and would not accept a passive role as obedient subjects [294]. Fully familiar with the participatory political culture of neighbouring Poland-Lithuania, they harboured a perception of Hohenzollern integration policies which differed greatly from that of Huguenots immigrants, who looked to a powerful ruler to protect their religion (see Chapter 2).

The suggestion by historians of east-central Europe that the estates, rather than the princes, were a modernising force, who promoted efficient structures and 'state-building' from the bottom up provides a rather different model which might be applied fruitfully to Brandenburg-Prussia [116, 143]. During the sixteenth century, the estates in most Hohenzollern territories understood their own role both as advisers of the ruler, and as an active corporate body which could take over the government in the case of the ruler's incapacity or absence abroad. This put the estates, particularly their most eminent members, into an awkward double role: appointed as the ruler's administrators and governors, they also acted as agents for the corporate estates, sometimes in opposition to the prince. But they also had a chance to mediate and find a compromise. At the same time, the estates gained the role of a legal body representing the country in whose entire name they negotiated and took decisions, most importantly on defence and taxation. In estate assemblies where native noblemen with local roots also acted as princely councillors, cooperation between the ruler's authority and the powers of the land often succeeded. Where the *ius indigenatus* (the exclusion of foreigners from landed properties and offices) was more blatantly violated, however, conflicts developed more openly.

Competition for truly representative guardianship over the land and the people was not devoid of patriotic motivation. The idea of birth, associated with noble virtue and service to the fatherland, was deeply ingrained in the estates' self-image. This perspective is often ignored in the debate on absolutism: the noble and urban estates could and frequently did develop an understanding of the common good (*bonum commune*) of their respective fatherlands and rallied behind it. Legitimacy, in the eyes of the estates, was closely connected to the rule of law – not the new law of necessity, as promoted by the ruler, but old law which the patriot defended in the interest of his commonweal (*res publica*) [119]. If the ruler's officials were recruited from abroad, they had other interests in mind and could not be trusted to be patriotic citizens. Responding to such views, rulers tried hard to establish their credentials as 'fathers of the fatherland', usually without specifying whether that title related to each historic province or the sum of all these smaller 'fatherlands' under their rule. The Hohenzollerns and their officials adeptly appropriated the rhetoric of the common good and patriotic council, seeking to supplant the estates as guardians of the common good [95].

When comparing the system in Brandenburg-Prussia with parliamentary models of representation in east-central Europe, the withering of the estates' participatory functions in the Hohenzollern territories is a noticeable trend from the late sixteenth century. In the mixed constitutions of east-central Europe the estates claimed a substantial share in legislative matters and exercised considerable control over their rulers: augmented by elected delegations from the provincial and local assemblies they set taxation, limited royal power to declare war, passed laws and sat in law courts over their peers and their subjects [114, 36, 140]. Part of the Prussian nobility tried to emulate the Polish example of open, parliamentary debate and dissent. Structural similarities between the two systems, however, should not conceal the obvious differences in political practice and culture. Poland-Lithuania lived under an elective monarchy, from 1573 chosen by the assembled nobility of the realm on an election field outside Warsaw. Hohenzollern political leadership was hereditary, which prevented the estates during interregna (the period between the death of one king and the election and coronation of his successor) to pass conditions to which the future ruler had to sign up if he wanted to be elected and crowned. Estates in hereditary systems had instead to rely on the presentation of supplications and grievances alone. In contrast to the Polish Senate, the members of the equivalent *Oberrat* (Supreme Council) in Prussia had to work their way up the administrative and political ladder: they could only enter the council after occupying one of the influential district offices (*Hauptamt*), whereas Polish senators could rise from the lesser nobility by royal appointment. Prussian district councillors (*Landräte*), representing the nobility in the provincial assembly, had a second face as salaried officials at the ducal court, which limited their political independence, in contrast to Poland-Lithuania, where the deputies to the Diet (*Sejm*) were bound by instructions by the local noble assemblies that elected them.

A country's political culture is formed by the way its political structures operate. Ducal Prussian assembly protocols are much less revealing than Polish ones. Little detail was recorded, as minutes were taken and kept by the ducal representatives, unlike in Poland, where parliamentary debates were conducted in public, and many diaries of diet sessions survive. Consensual politics in Prussia only permitted general protestations in formulaic language. In contrast to the open language of debate in Polish diet sessions, the members of Prussian estate assemblies, particularly in the lower chamber, hesitated to discuss their rights in detail, afraid it would invite close scrutiny. In 1662 the estates argued that open debate would only weaken their rights, as anybody could 'cast doubt on them and drag our well-founded privileges and immunities into dispute' [75; 171–92]. None of the diets in the Brandenburg-Prussian territories, including Ducal Prussia, ever possessed powers that resembled the political autonomy and the legal position of the noble estates in the Polish Sejm. Most significantly the Brandenburg-Prussian estates never had a united representative body until 1847.

This explains why the Hohenzollerns found themselves in a situation of constant communication with local bodies, moulding their policies by adapting them to the separate circumstances in each province. Starting, however, from a less limited constitutional position than the Polish kings, they ultimately succeeded in minimising or even abolishing the participatory institutions which had flourished in their territories in the fifteenth and sixteenth centuries. Because of this need to differentiate between the provinces, Brandenburg-Prussia's composite character makes it difficult to talk about an all-embracing governmental style of 'absolutism', but we should be careful not to take revisionism too far. Many nobles spoke with hostility of 'absolute government' (*absolutum dominium*), just as Polish nobles attacked their monarch for 'absolute' tendencies [140; 147–67].

[ii] Noble Power in the Composite *Ständestaat*

In their testaments Hohenzollern rulers demonstrated an awareness of their nobles' different regional backgrounds. The Great Elector recommended keeping an eye on the Ducal Prussian estates, admonishing his heir to 'flatter the Prussians but always watch them carefully', while praising the estates in Brandenburg for their loyalty. Frederick William I distinguished even more clearly between the Pomeranians, who were 'faithful as gold', the Prussians, who were a 'false and cunning *nacion*', the Magdeburg nobility which, as in the Altmark, had proved 'disobedient', while the inhabitants of Minden and Ravensberg were 'dumb and opinionated'; the most obstinate, however, were the Cleves nobles, whose nature was also 'malicious' [225]. Frederick II only adjusted these characterisations marginally. Such tirades against the estates' stubborn resistance were, however, accompanied by a clear analysis of each province's institutional, economic and religious circumstances. A closer look at these provinces will underline the necessity of thinking about the Brandenburg-Prussian nobility as a heterogeneous group which responded in widely different ways to their rulers' schemes for closer union. What follows are selected examples illustrating the estates' responses and their interaction with Hohenzollern policies across the dynasty's expanding territories. The examples are discussed in the chronological order of their acquisition and incorporation by the Hohenzollerns: Brandenburg (1417), Ducal Prussia (1525), Cleves-Mark (1614), Ravensberg (1647), Pomerania (1648), Minden and Halberstadt (1648), Magdeburg (1648/1680) (see Map 3). Examples of eighteenth-century acquisitions, such as Silesia (1740) and the Prussian partitions of Poland (1772, 1793, 1795) are discussed in chapter 5 (see Maps 5 and 6).

Despite continuous Hohenzollern rule from 1415, when the Emperor installed burgrave Frederick of Nuremberg as the first Hohenzollern Elector in **Brandenburg**, the character of its provinces, the Electoral Mark (comprising Altmark, Mittelmark, Uckermark and Prignitz), and after 1463 Neumark (with Sternberg, Crossen, Züllichau and Cottbus), varied greatly (see Map 1). In Neumark influences from Silesia and Bohemia ensured the survival of strong noble estates, regular diets and provincial dietines which negotiated effectively with the rulers in Berlin [131; xvii–xix]. In the Electoral Mark, Hohenzollern attempts to mitigate the initial hostility of powerful local noble clans had been protracted but increasingly successful during the fifteenth and early sixteenth centuries [8; I 36–41, 82].

Due to his enormous debts, Elector Joachim II had to rely on close cooperation with the estates. As the prince's principal creditors, the estates secured their influence over foreign policy. In tandem with the Brandenburg treasury, the chancellery and the financial administration of the court, the *Kreditwerk*, an estate-controlled, provincial finance institution, continued to exist well into the nineteenth century [73, 59; 41–79]. Throughout the early modern period, therefore, the Brandenburg estates created and maintained their own institutions, sharing government with the ruler, reflecting a complexity too easily concealed by the catch-all phrase of 'state-building' [59; 389].

One example of the politics of compromise so typical of Brandenburg were Frederick William's negotiations with the provincial estates over the introduction of an excise tax on agricultural and manufacturing products to support a permanent army to secure the post-Westphalian acquisition of Pomerania. Brandenburg had grown accustomed to such demands. Reduced committees or deputy diets had become the accepted forum for policy-making earlier than in other territories [16; 255–61, 75; 53–76]. In 1652, in order to press his demands, the Elector called the first full assembly since 1615. He had spent much of 1651–2 in his other territories, mostly pursuing the integration of Cleves-Mark. He had left Brandenburg governed by a council and a governor who were ineffective in securing the agreement of the estates to the Elector's demands. Only when he returned to Berlin in 1653 did he negotiate a settlement both sides could accept. The significance of the Brandenburg Recess of 1653 has often been interpreted as a watershed in the relationship between the ruler and his estates who agreed to pass a contribution of 530,000 thalers to buy back alienated domains to finance fortresses and a peacetime army, dropping their initial demands for military retrenchment [16; 431–3]. In return for this commitment, the Elector confirmed noble exemption from excise and custom tolls, burdening cities and towns instead. Although the estates were keen to stress that the Recess had not set a precedent, its significance only becomes clear in hindsight: when two years later the Second Northern War broke out between Poland-Lithuania and Sweden, the Elector successfully argued 'necessity' to turn the one-off tax agreement into a permanent contribution. In contrast to older historiography which stressed the restrictive impact of the imperial constitution on Prussia's rise to power, in this instance the Empire assisted Frederick William. He successfully used his influence in the Imperial Diet to secure an imperial law in 1654, ruling that the princes' subjects had to 'contribute helpfully to [the prince's] necessary fortifications and garrisons' [18].

Not all of the Elector's territories were subject to imperial regulation. Greater traditional liberties, but also greater conflicts existed in **Ducal Prussia**, whose increasing integration into the wider European economy had given rise to prosperous nobles and towns, above all the city of Königsberg. The grain-exporting Junkers benefited from high demand for their products in northern Europe and accumulated extensive financial means [192]. Like Joachim, Albrecht borrowed heavily from the estates to finance his newly-created secular court [76]. Although the Order had been the largest landowner, controlling over 60 per cent of the land, it had accumulated large debts. As the ruler's main creditors, the local nobles had benefited from a transfer of landed properties, a tendency that continued after secularisation [67; 127–8, 180, 196]. The Ducal Prussian estates acquired privileges which nobles in Brandenburg could only dream of, such as considerable political influence through their Diet (*Landtag*), the right of lower and higher jurisdiction and extensive patronage rights.

The most important document for the Prussian estates was the *Regimentsnottel* of 1542, which the estates considered the fundamental law of the duchy, and to which they turned in defence of their privileges. In exchange for much needed taxation, Duke Albrecht had guaranteed the *ius indigenatus*, the rule of law, and other privileges which existed in similar form in other territories under Hohenzollern rule. The *Regimentsnottel* did not, however, introduce a Polish-style free election, the constitutional right of resistance, or the sovereignty of the *Landtag*. Yet through the feudal relationship of 1525, the Prussian estates had de facto two rulers, a suzerain lord (the Polish king) and his vassal (the duke), whom they tried to play off against each other. This triangular relationship gave the Prussian estates a fierce political confidence.

Not all Polish policies were in the Prussian estates' interest. This became evident in 1578, when a Polish commission invested duke Albrecht's unpopular nephew, margrave George Frederick, with stewardship over the duchy. After George Frederick's death in 1603, king Sigismund III granted the right of stewardship to the Brandenburg line in the duchy, dashing any hopes that Ducal Prussia might be reunited with its western part under the Polish crown. In 1618, after the death of the long-incapacitated Albert Frederick (see Appendix 1), Hohenzollern succession to the duchy became hereditary in the electoral branch against the protests of a group of nobles under the leadership of Otto von Gröben. The influence of his pro-Polish faction diminished only when it became clear that the Polish king wanted to quarter troops in the country. The king's popularity might have suffered, but Polish noble liberties remained attractive. In 1658, a year after the Elector negotiated sovereignty from the Polish crown, the Prussian chancellor Otto von Schwerin wearily wrote to his master: 'Your Electoral Highness would not believe to what extent the Polish crown is dear to their hearts and how they all seek their advantage in this connection, so that they insist on maintaining some recourse to Poland. As long as one generation lives who remembers Polish rule, there will be a source of resistance in Prussia.' Schwerin's advice to treat them with leniency remained unheeded [137, 118].

Consequently, many nobles and *Kölmer* (free non-noble landowners) boycotted the 1663 oath of allegiance to Frederick William. The von Schlieben and von Kreytzen families, most prominent among the refuseniks, were threatened with a fine of 200 thalers. Administrators and subjects from over 15 *Ämter* absented themselves or refused to swear their oath, despite being threatened with confiscation of their properties. Repeated orders from 1663 and 1664 show little reaction to such posturing. In Memel, the church elders and citizenry avoided paying homage until after 1707 [62, 127; 100].

One case gained particular notoriety. Christian Ludwig von Kalckstein, after being fined by the ducal court over a family dispute, fled to Warsaw where he accused the Elector of tyranny and 'foreign occupation' [135]. Kalckstein was rolled up in a carpet, abducted by ducal agents, and executed – in a violation of all noble immunities. As late as 1722, Frederick William I advised his successor to watch the Prussian noble families carefully, since they 'keep the old Prussian Polish privileges in their hearts' [225; 229].

If the peripatetic Hohenzollern ruler found it difficult to control affairs in the east, he experienced a similarly rough start to the relationship with his new subjects in the distant west. As in Prussia, resistance to centralising tendencies was widespread among the nobles of **Cleves, Mark and Ravensberg** due to another foreign constitutional model: Dutch republican ideas were popular both with the estates and the Elector's advisers in the Cleves governing council [126]. In a treatise Nikolaus Langenberg (1573–1628), one of Brandenburg's councillors on the Lower Rhine, depicted the Dutch nation as a positive example for displaying civic courage in repelling the Habsburgs [117]. In 1616 Langenberg served in a delegation from Cleves and Mark to present grievances to their overlord in Königsberg. Their criticism was directed at the mass dismissals of Cleves officials by the Elector and the ruler's perpetual absence, with the result that policy-making was delegated to lower-ranking officials who pursued their private interests. In an appeal to knightly virtues, they called for an end to foreign occupation of the fatherland, leaving the meaning of 'foreign' open to interpretation. In defending their right of self-assembly, the estates saw themselves as guardians of the common good. Langenberg, a Catholic, recommended a policy of religious toleration and pointedly discussed the right of resistance. For his labours he was put under house arrest for two years, while the grievances remained unaddressed. Yet the Cleves estates maintained a diplomatic envoy to the Hague until 1660 [117; 68–81].

In contrast to his behaviour in Prussia after 1657, the Elector relented in Cleves-Mark, partly due to the imperial context which restricted his actions, partly with respect to the Dutch alliance. In 1647 the ring-fencing of provincial autonomies persuaded the Cleves estates to pass a financial settlement in the Elector's favour. Military excesses by the Brandenburg military commander against the cities sparked renewed conflict in 1650–2. The ringleader of a deputation from Cleves, which lodged an appeal to the Imperial Diet in Regensburg, was the Catholic nobleman Dietrich Karl von Wilich of Winnenthal, renowned as a fierce defender of provincial political autonomy. Using confessional and political differences among the Cleves-Mark estates in 1654, the Elector had Winnenthal arrested, imprisoned in Spandau, and his properties confiscated.

Frederick William succeeded in reaching a compromise with the nobility, by 1655 deprived of Dutch protection. The appointment of local councillors with pro-Brandenburg leanings, who benefited from a policy of cooperation with the Elector, bore fruit. They agreed, in 1660, to abolish the participation of the estates in the setting of taxation levels [126]. Due to an insecure international situation, the estates accepted a more direct style of government and the contributions that accompanied it, accepting the Elector's interpretation of the 'common good'. As in Prussia, public controversy was considered illegitimate and prone to devalue constitutional norms: grievances were presented but not openly discussed. This explains the arcane nature of many early modern assembly protocols.

A rather different situation presented itself in the former ecclesiastical territories of the Empire acquired at the Peace of Westphalia. The secularised bishoprics of **Minden** and **Halberstadt** were granted to Brandenburg-Prussia as compensation for its failure to obtain the whole of Pomerania from the Swedes. Minden became a secular duchy in 1648, but, bound by the Articles of Westphalia which fixed the confessional distribution of imperial territories according to the status quo in 1624, the Elector had to retain the confessionally-mixed cathedral chapter in Minden, which survived

Estate Society and Life in the Rural Economy

until 1810. In 1719, Minden was merged with the neighbouring county of Ravensberg and its capital Bielefeld, with its profitable linen trade and manufacturing industry. Ravensberg had belonged to Jülich-Cleves and became a Hohenzollern possession in 1647. Minden and Ravensberg were administered by one centrally-appointed governor and subject to a joint War and Domain Chamber from 1723 [117].

The former bishopric could hardly compensate for the strategic and economic gains which the whole of Pomerania would have brought. Minden's estates, which paid homage to the new Hohenzollern ruler in 1650, were dominated by the lower nobility of a small curia of knights and monastic prelates. The corporate traditions lived on relatively undisturbed until 1674, when the Elector demanded payment of the excise. The estates' direct control over their finances was transferred in 1678 to a commissariat collecting contributions. As the excise failed to produce the expected return, it was restricted to the cities after 1682/3. Although the estates did not regain their right of self-taxation, Minden and Ravensberg kept most of their local institutional and legal structures, which minimised conflicts with the central authorities in Berlin. The Elector also trod more cautiously, since in all Rhenish and Westphalian territories the estates maintained close contacts to their peers in Cleves, Jülich-Berg and to the Dutch occupation forces which remained on the Rhine until the 1670s.

Integration was here a calmer, more gradual process than in Ducal Prussia and Cleves. As in his other territories, the Elector introduced local governors and centrally appointed officials into the provincial councils of Minden and Halberstadt, where membership from the former bishoprics was marginal. In Halberstadt, the district councillors retained a link of communication between the government council and the estates, but lost direct participation rights. After the 1690s, provincial political life continued in local noble assemblies within established structures that changed little in the countryside, but the estates lost influence over the central budget, foreign policy, and legislation.

The prince bishopric of **Magdeburg** had been an object of Hohenzollern ambitions since the sixteenth century, when the chapter had repeatedly elected members of the dynasty as bishops. After Sigismund of Hohenzollern introduced the Reformation in 1561, secular administrators co-ruled the bishopric with the chapter and the landed estates. It was assigned to Brandenburg in 1648, but incorporation had to be postponed until the current Saxon administrator died in 1680, when the introduction of hereditary Hohenzollern rule meant that the chapter lost its right of election. Aspiring to free imperial status, the city of Madgeburg refused homage to the new lord, but could not sustain its opposition. Threatened by Frederick William's troops, it submitted to his government and received a garrison [59; 170–207]. The landed estates in Magdeburg were dominated by a few powerful families, who relied on their territories outside the former bishopric and were used to serving in foreign armies. As in Minden and Halberstadt, Magdeburg diets summoned themselves, but a reform of its so-called Great Deputation Assembly soon gave the Elector influence over its composition. In a familiar pattern, Madgeburg's privileges were eroded through the excise (1685/6), the Tax Directory of 1692, and taxation without consultation from around 1708. By 1713, Frederick William I introduced the Magdeburg Commissariat, which abolished the estates' direct financial management [75; 77–98]. The estates still had recourse to the Emperor through a system of appeals, which, although rarely successful, had a psychological impact on the Hohenzollerns. It was used against Frederick William I's allodification programme in 1714–17 and caused him a few sleepless nights, despite the estates' ultimate failure to prevent the implementation of his policies.

The **Pomeranian** nobility also boasted a strong autonomous political tradition. The originally Slavonic dynasty ended with duke Bogislav XIV's death in 1637. Although Frederick William held guaranteed succession rights to the duchy, he had to surrender them to Sweden during the Osnabrück peace negotiations, despite strong support from the so-called Pomeranian 'patriot party' [59; 155–69]. He merely secured the poorer parts of eastern Pomerania and the bishopric of Cammin which the Swedes finally evacuated in 1653–4. After 1657, the Hohenzollerns exploited Sweden's numerous wars to secure ever more Pomeranian territory until Sweden's last foothold was annexed in 1815 [24, 115].

As the country had suffered badly during the Thirty Years War, Frederick William knew that he could not replenish his coffers there. Yet he insisted on expanding his garrison in Kolberg. The fortress housed the seat of the provincial government, which was composed of native officials with good knowledge of the provincial traditions. Although the Elector appointed his officeholders himself, his choices were limited by the Pomeranian version of the *ius indigenatus*: hereditary offices remained in the hands of the native elites. Modelled on its equivalent in other Hohenzollern territories, the *Amtskammer*, or governing chamber, was introduced to administer the domains and the provincial landed economy under the Elector's direct authority.

At first glance, Frederick William's careful approach caused relatively little friction with the estates, in contrast to the situation in Ducal Prussia or Cleves, where he swiftly removed negotiations about fundamental laws and the contractual nature of rulership from the agenda. Many of the novelties introduced elsewhere, such as the estates' loss of the right of appeal to imperial courts, allodification and the establishment of provincial commissariats, failed to make an impact in eastern Pomerania until the later eighteenth century. The strong Lutheran tradition of the estates also kept the influx of Calvinists to a minimum, although some prominent Pomeranian families, such as the von Krockow, converted. Swedish competition for Pomerania meant that the Elector had to tread carefully on religion; this guaranteed the survival of the local estates' participatory prerogatives more effectively than Polish influence in Prussia or Dutch presence in Cleves, even after 1679 and 1715, when further parts of Swedish Pomerania fell to Prussia. The Hohenzollerns knew that the Swedes meant business, at least until their great power status began to decline dramatically after 1709.

Not all territorial examples can be included here, but throughout the seventeenth and early eighteenth centuries certain patterns emerge. Göse's research on the Brandenburg nobility suggests that the Hohenzollerns were more effective than other German princes in reducing their estates' participatory rights, and that the intense mobilisation of financial resources accompanying that process was only achieved through the impoverishment and decline of some of the oldest families. They bitterly resented that leading positions at the court, in the army and the growing bureaucracy were filled with noblemen from Hohenzollern territories other than their own. This exchange of noble elites was partly deliberate, but also a consequence of the alienation of Lutheran nobles by John Sigismund's conversion in 1613, the economic impact of war, the forced sale of families' patrimonial properties to rich newcomers, and the ruler's decisive centralisation policies to fill the power vacuum created by the weakening of traditional elites [182; 75; 53–76]. On the other hand, after the crisis of the seventeenth century, career opportunities for nobles outside the landed economy were vital to the survival of heavily-indebted families who were facing the ruin of their estates, in some areas barely sustained by a substantially reduced labour-force. The creativity of the nobility, who knew conditions in the countryside well, and their civic engagement for their province have too often been ignored: many more detailed, local studies are needed to fill this gap. What Hagen has shown for Stavenow and the Altmark, Neugebauer for East Prussia, Motsch for Draheim, and Hahn and Göse for Brandenburg and Neumark, are the first steps towards a more comprehensive picture of Brandenburg-Prussian noble elites, their relation to their rulers and to their rural subjects.

The nobility, even within one territory, was not a homogenous group. The role of the ruler's army as employer for impoverished noblemen gained increasing significance. Such a service function became a highly valued career option, especially for younger sons unlikely to inherit fortunes sufficient to enable them to continue their ancestors' lifestyle. The result was the creation of a military service class which secured status built on a consensus between ruler, his growing political apparatus, and the noble estates. Religious differences drew new battle lines, and in some cases attracted a small aristocratic Calvinist elite to the court. Many nobles from small territories with modest career opportunities sought their fortune in Berlin, benefiting from the Electors' willingness to appoint in breach of the *ius indigenatus*. The eighteenth-century monarchs cultivated this service nobility. Frederick II's policy of protecting the nobility helped whole clans survive on advantageous credit [190; 257–86].

In their role of social and political elites the noble estates presented a valued force of commitment and innovation for the territorial ruler. Prussian nobles, for example, suggested an arrangement closely resembling the Kanton system long before Frederick William I introduced it [182; 212–20]. Noblemen who knew local conditions wrote regular memoranda on melioration projects, and communicated legislative initiatives via the dense network of Ämter and district councillors. Obstructive petitions and grievances were not the only way to raise issues. Constructive criticism and modernising change emanated from the estates themselves in many ways, both in their ruling function and as representatives of their lands.

Did this amount to 'absolutism'? Absolutism might have been a political theory beloved by the princes. Princely reform was not, however, imposed on a passive albeit privileged class, but practiced in collaboration with the estates, based on the concept of a shared fatherland and its common good, though sometimes this was defined by both sides in conflicting terms. If we wish to maintain the concept of absolutism, as Wilson has recommended, we must also follow his advice not to reduce its meaning to an abstract model of rule and subjection [112; 121–3]. The ruler's exclusive claim to absolute rule as a phenomenon of modernisation must be disputed for Brandenburg-Prussia, especially if we consider this conglomerate of territories in the context of the wider liberty-traditions of the east-central European 'state of estates' (*Ständestaat*). Modernisation could not have worked without their participation and active involvement.

[iii] *Gutsherrschaft*

The landed estates of the western Empire were run differently from those situated east of the Elbe. This division has dominated the discussion of much of Germany's early modern agrarian history. While in the western Empire, estates were often administered by absentee landlords through cash rent systems, and the landed population was personally free, the estates east of the Elbe were generally ruled by *Gutsherrschaft*, which gave the landlord power to interfere directly in the lives of their subjects [5; 111–28,188]. Liselott Enders differentiated three forms of *Gutsherrschaft*: rule over subjects who submitted to seigniorial domination on a contractual basis; subjects, who inherited their servile status and handed it on to their children; and hereditary serfs, who were bound to the land and could only buy themselves free with the landlord's consent [181].

The seigniorial estate tended to be run by the noble family living on the demesne land, where labour was tenured through various legal and economic contracts. In the later sixteenth century, the legal conditions of the Prussian peasantry (including the German, non-Pruzzen population) deteriorated, despite Duke Albrecht's decree that there should only be free subjects who 'would work the land more eagerly, while rent and farms would not suffer damage' [224; 198–9]. Cases of binding Prussian serfs to their landlord's person, who could sell or buy them, were not unknown [196; 436]. Albrecht encouraged Prussian serfs to train to be church ministers who could preach in Prussian and Lithuanian, and those who took up theological studies did acquire personal freedom, but this only affected a few. Tenants under Kulm or German law usually owned their houses and gardens, but they had to provide a substitute tenant if they wished to move away. Although hereditary Pruzzen serfs were bound to the glebe and banned from crafts and residence in Kulm-law villages, they could acquire, own, inherit and bequeath property to their families. Householders formed a village community which was recognised as a legal personality, which had the right to litigate against oppressive seigniorial measures.

These liberties were further curtailed when the Ducal Prussian constitution of 1577 introduced the obligation of tenants' children to serve the lord of the manor before they could move away or take over their parents' homestead and land. The Prussian cities refused to return fugitive peasants' sons who fled to the city to settle, learn crafts and marry into burgher society. The service burden seems to have peaked at that point in many territories of northeast Germany, with around two or three days per week of demesne labour in Brandenburg, which in most cases was done by hired or landless labourers or younger family members without their own homestead.

The devastation caused by the wars of the seventeenth century was reflected in the desertion of farmland, which in most cases in Brandenburg (up to 80 per cent in the Mittelmark) and parts of Ducal Prussia had been in the villagers' possession [199; 145–90]. Although landlords tried to integrate these vacant territories into their own estates, the shortage of labour gave villagers in many places a bargaining power which reversed the less advantageous contracts they had been forced to accept during the late sixteenth century. As a result, rents fell and contracts became more favourable for farm tenants willing and able to assist reconstruction. Fierce competition for labour ruled out the imposition of legal coercion and excessive duties, which before the wars had exacerbated the problem of peasant flight to the towns or across the border, particularly to Poland, where they could sometimes settle as free farmers [189; 40–2, 199; 176].

Conflicts intensified towards the end of the seventeenth century, when landlords tried to return to pre-1618 conditions, imposing more burdensome labour dues and conditions. The Prussian Land Law of 1685 made the deterioration of the privileges of formerly free tenants permanent by abolishing the special classification of Kulm-law tenants, who were now generally called 'peasants', on a par with their less privileged Prussian peers [196; 458]. It was not in Ducal Prussia, however, but in Brandenburg's Uckermark that the most oppressive conditions prevailed; here in 1653 the local nobility surrendered self-taxation in exchange for the right to impose severe servile conditions upon their manorial subjects [20; 225–42]. Uckermark subjects got an exceptionally rough deal, as their right to inherit was turned into the duty to remain in the same manorial service, while the lord of the manor gained the right to expel rebellious peasants [148; 146–8].

The concentration of such judicial and economic powers over the subject population gave *Gutsherrschaft* a bad name. Measures which have been considered particularly oppressive include the prohibition of departure without seigniorial approval, the serfs' obligation to provide paid or unpaid labour to the landowner and send their children to work at the manor house. This system, which is presumed to have functioned on the basis of noble-ruler cooperation against the landed population, groaning under a double burden of landlord exploitation and heavy state taxation, has long been interpreted as lying behind nineteenth-century Germany's economic backwardness [177, 187, 198].

The revision of several aspects of Germany's historical *Sonderweg* since the 1980s has opened up the social and economic history of the East Elbian territories to new questions which have encouraged a whole range of detailed case studies on lord-subject relations. Hagen has shown that behind the labels of 'Junkers' and 'peasants' hides a reality of both bureaucratisation and commercialisation which is difficult to categorise [184; 122]. In contrast to the traditional picture of the East-Elbian landed economy in the grip of the Junker class, who imposed an ever stricter regime of 'neo-serfdom', Hagen found that Brandenburg landlords implemented technical and managerial innovations by applying the know-how of commercially astute estate administrators. It is no longer possible to speak summarily about the powers that ruled the land in Brandenburg-Prussia as cut off from wider European developments [194].

Another approach has stressed that the picture of double oppression, associated with the rise of 'absolute' government after 1648, looks less conclusive if conflicting interests between noble landowners and territorial rulers are taken into account. If the prince wished to collect as much taxation and to recruit as many able-bodied soldiers from the land as possible, the local lord of the manor sought to protect his labour force and his sources of income. The landlord appreciated the state's policing and disciplining powers, but certainly objected when his wealth was siphoned off by the ruler's tax collectors and armies.

Thus it was in the nobility's interest to look after its peasantry. Large parts of the Brandenburg-Prussian labour force were more restrained by tenancy obligations than its western counterpart, but there was a trade-off: East Elbian subjects might have been less free, but not as poor as some of their rural contemporaries in the south-west of the Empire, where the massive peasant revolts that had followed Luther's religious reform movement in 1525 abolished serfdom but did not necessarily lift peasants out of poverty.

Religious and reformist ideas could also affect individual landowners' attitudes to their subject population. Strong Calvinist beliefs are reflected in the four Dohna brothers' 1621 testament, in which they stipulated that their successors must 'treat their subjects in a Christian and moderate way, because they have to consider that Our Lord and Saviour shed his blood not only for the powerful of this world, but also for the most humble and poor man'. Heide Wunder warns against the cynical dismissal of such statements. The Dohnas' beliefs went beyond a simple patriarchal vision of rulership over their subjects, as is shown in a similar testament of 1652, granting personal freedom to serfs and subjects who had served the manor loyally for 'six to eight years' [201; 229–30].

Less wealthy landowners often had to demonstrate a pragmatic and imaginative economic sense to overcome periods of crisis. Monetary exchange, rent income and paid labour sustained the manorial economy as much as labour services and payment in kind. The contractual nature of relationships encouraged a range of enterprises: a sales-oriented agrarian production, industry and crafts in villages which ran their own local markets [201]. The existence of such activities suggests that cash wages must have played a role throughout the early modern period, giving the local population opportunities beyond exchange in kind, and a limited autonomy [184; 184–279].

By the early eighteenth century there is evidence of widespread commutation of labour service into cash quitrent. If that gave tenants a chance to become more mobile, many rent-paying tenants still could not pay their way to independence: without property to sell, they could not raise enough money to buy their freedom. Royal protection policies for serfs on royal estates in 1718/19 showed little direct results, although the harsher forms of servile labour thereafter diminished steadily, even in Uckermark, due to demographic growth, developing commercial activities and increasing peasant prosperity [25; 388–9].

Much more research needs to be done into the socio-economic complexities of the Brandenburg-Prussian countryside. At present we can mainly discern patterns influenced by local traditions and conditions. Sources from the mid-eighteenth century show that around 60 per cent of Ducal Prussia's subjects did not owe any labour services, or less than one day's work per week, although around 20 per cent of the subject population did owe heavy labour services of five or more days a week – evidence that the situation for the landed subject population varied greatly even within one province, casting some doubt on the validity of a unitary model of east-Elbian *Gutsherrschaft*.

Microhistory and anthropological research have inspired a group of researchers combining the best traditions of social history in the former East Germany and western Europe to focus on strategies of popular resistance. Jan Peters, Heinrich Kaak, Enders, Wunder, and others queried traditional assumptions concerning peasant passivity and submission, thereby undermining the smooth story of success associated with the social power of the East Elbian nobility [186, 193, 194, 195]. The new agrarian history has taken particular care to resurrect from the archives the lives of the common people, largely ignored by traditional economic history and structural approaches to 'state-building'. Degraded to the status of passive victims – a view reinforced by the absence of major peasant rebellions – there had been no historical interest in less spectacular acts of resistance, which *Alltagsgeschichte* (history of everyday life) now revealed [184, 199].

Control over peasants' lives was hampered by litigation and uneasy compromises. The lives and the economic value of Brandenburg-Prussian subjects were not only important to their immediate manorial lords. By introducing cameralist principles and policies of 'peasant protection', the Hohenzollerns aimed at sustaining a prosperous population for taxation purposes and the augmentation of the army, a goal sometimes consciously exploited by the subjects against local landlords' demands. 'Motives of self-preservation and self-interest' seem to have dominated on all sides and created overall a precarious but functioning balance, not built on harmony but conflict [184; 591].

The result was not a Prussian *Sonderweg*. In sixteenth-century Europe, where taxation and dues in kind differed widely across European agrarian economies, Brandenburg peasants were burdened in a roughly equal measure to the peasants of Languedoc; they fared better than the rural population in Russia or around Paris, and worse than peasants in Poland, where legal structures were comparable to their own, but where no powerful central ruler intervened in the noble-subject relationship. Peasant dues in Brandenburg, Upper Swabia and Languedoc amounted to between 23 and 25 per cent of the provinces' overall returns in grain production, while Parisian and Muscovite peasants paid 40 per cent, and Polish subjects only 10 per cent. The net amount handed over in tax and manorial dues in Brandenburg and Poland was practically equal – around 700 kg of grain – but in Poland productivity was better, as this 10 per cent was produced on an average-sized property of 16.8 ha of arable land. In Brandenburg, 700 kg of grain amounted to 23.5 per cent of the return from an almost equal-sized average property [183]. According to these figures, Brandenburg subjects fared about the same as west German ones, while French and Muscovite subjects were worst off. This certainly explains the frequency in France and Russia of peasant uprisings, which were relatively rare in Poland and Brandenburg.

The question remains to what extent rural subjects identified with Prussia and its composite parts. Primary sources are rare, but we can glimpse some evidence from chronicles which show that identity was closely connected with the immediate locality, region or province, not necessarily targeted at Brandenburg-Prussia as a larger entity [300]. Even towards the late eighteenth century, local concerns prevailed over an interest in the person of the monarch or the state, unless these touched directly upon the village in the form of taxation or army billeting. Remarkably, there is an awareness of the larger entity of the Empire, which is reflected in numerous legal procedures submitted by rural communities and individuals to the imperial law court in Vienna [191, 194; 17–28]. The common name of 'Prussians', which Frederick II wanted to impose on all of his subjects and soldiers, remained above all associated with the original province of East Prussia, beyond the Empire's borders, where the Prussian crown had been founded in 1701.

The revival of the noble estates towards the end of the eighteenth century, first during the Seven Years War, but particularly after Frederick II's death in 1786, and throughout the Napoleonic period, also reinvigorated rural self-administration among village elites [20, 181]. Free rural subjects (*Kölmer*), who during the late seventeenth century had lost their position in the Ducal Prussian Landtag, still amounted to approximately 12 per cent of the rural population. District assemblies, the homage paid to the new ruler after 1786, the ritual submission of grievances, as well as discussions concerning the new General Legal Code for Prussia (1791/94) were marked by the physical presence of representatives of these freemen, although they had no independent voice or vote [191; 159]. A sense of common purpose is still hard to gauge from such events.

Revisionism should not go too far: neither the Hohenzollern government and its agents, nor the Prussian landlords were particularly philanthropic, nor in any way attracted to models of self-government among their subjects. If local voices were given a hearing, it was done in the interest of the powers of the landlord and for the prosperity of their estates. One must not ignore, therefore, the cameralist interest of landowners and the government in the well-being of their subjects, especially on family-run estates, whose prosperity was crucial for the economic survival of the elites and the state as a whole.

4 From Baroque Court to Military Monarchy

[i] Coronation

The nineteenth-century image of the frugal Prussian bureaucratic state has obscured the significance of its Baroque court which competed for dynastic rank and prestige after 1688. The Prussian monarchy was founded on 18 January 1701, when Elector Frederick III placed the royal crown on his own head as Frederick I, 'king in Prussia'. The coronation took place in Königsberg, far from Berlin and the Brandenburg heartlands, which would not become the centre of the monarchy until later in the eighteenth century [232, 331, 357]. The coronation was accompanied by a massive construction programme, involving the construction or renovation of palaces and monuments, the expansion of the University of Halle, founded in 1694, and the opening of the Society of Sciences in Berlin in 1700, all accompanied by a series of eye-catching ceremonies.

Historians traditionally criticised Frederick's ceremonial extravaganza [234]. His Baroque court has been depicted as a freak phenomenon and a quirky exception to the sober and rational way his successors conducted the propagation of their personae and power. This judgement was strongly influenced by Frederick II's quip that his grandfather was 'a ruler great in small things and small in great things', tempted by frivolous luxury and led astray by self-interested advisers.

Succeeding his father Frederick William as Elector in 1688, Frederick III – as he then was – knew very well, however, that a royal crown was symbolic capital worthy of investment on the European stage of Baroque monarchies. In the words of Heinrich Rüdiger von Ilgen, Frederick's trusted advisor who orchestrated the 1701 coronation, the objective was political recognition which would follow

From Baroque Court to Military Monarchy

the ceremonial exercise: 'It was not enough to be crowned; one needs to be assured that one will be recognised as a king' [251, 163; 548–59]. How was that achieved? This chapter looks at some of the approaches used by the new cultural history of politics to communicate the 'otherness' of early modern politics. Instead of dismissing Frederick's coronation and court building as 'a politics of empty gestures', we should ask how his ceremonial programme related to the dynasty's ambition and legitimacy. For it was not only the size of the army, military strategies and bureaucratic innovation that supported the rise of this composite state, but also symbols and rituals that were turned into tools of power politics [13; 14–35].

The revision of Frederick's negative image is echoed in Neugebauer's emphasis on the continuities of Prussia's administrative and military policies from the Great Elector to Frederick William I [242]. Other revisionist portraits have, in comparison to other German princes, emphasised Frederick I's relatively modest spending on the court. While Bavaria spent 1.35 million thalers in 1701, Prussia's court expenditure in the record year of 1711/12 amounted to around a third of that: 421,000 thalers [220]. Saxony trumped them both, rivalling the Habsburg dynasty as it sought to establish a court of European significance and true royal status after 1697 – partly through the personal union with Poland-Lithuania, and partly due to the Wettin dynasty's abundant resources [255].

After 1648, the imperial constitution allowed its princes greater political autonomy, but within the Empire it still reserved royal status to the imperial house. Princes who wished to add a royal title needed a territorial base beyond the Empire's jurisdiction. It was now that the importance of the sovereignty in Ducal Prussia secured in 1657 (see Chapter 5) became clear. The electors of Brandenburg knew that elevation above other princes in the Empire presented the ultimate path to peer recognition. Throughout the seventeenth century, they had failed to achieve this goal: perceived as a second-rate power, Brandenburg-Prussia continued to be ill-treated by ceremonial protocol and snubbed at European courts which gave Venice, Tuscany and Savoy precedence over the Electorate. Such behaviour had heightened Brandenburg-Prussia's sense of insecurity.

Frederick's rivals, however, had similar ideas: Frederick August of Saxony converted to Catholicism in 1697 to win the election to the Polish royal throne, the Elector of Bavaria unsuccessfully sought the Spanish crown in the 1690s, while the house of Hanover was raised to an electorate in 1692 and secured the succession to the English throne in 1701 [258, 227; 1–52]. Frederick's pursuit of monarchic status was no vainglorious whim, but the result of eminently rational politics.

Habsburg consent was indispensible. Frederick exploited Emperor Leopold's need for allies against France in the approaching conflict for the Spanish Succession to negotiate the 1700 *Krontraktat*: in exchange for Brandenburg auxiliary troops, Leopold withdrew his objections to Ducal Prussia becoming a kingdom. The gamble paid off. In 1702 when Brandenburg troops marched against France the maritime powers not only sided against France but also paid subsidies to Berlin [238; 229–55, 278; 110–17].

Not all his neighbours gave Frederick such an easy ride. Although the king of Poland and Elector of Saxony Augustus the Strong formally acknowledged the foundation of the Prussian monarchy, the Polish-Lithuanian Diet refused its consent and declared the coronation of 1701 illegal, contesting Frederick's right to accept a crown of a province which they believed still belonged to the Polish Crown. A clause in the treaty of Wehlau and Bromberg of 1657 stipulated that Ducal Prussia would revert to Poland if the Brandenburg Hohenzollerns died out in the direct male line. The Elector's sovereignty therefore was not absolute, but depended on a regular succession of male heirs. This reversionary right called into question the Elector's right to elevate Prussia into a monarchy. Official accounts of the coronation, including Johannes von Besser's *History of the Prussian Coronation*, fail to mention this restriction [222]. It explains, however, why Frederick had to accept the title 'king in Prussia' (instead of 'king of Prussia') as a concession to Polish objections. Historians are wrong to ignore the significance of Frederick's intense but unsuccessful efforts to win over the Polish nobility [274, 233]. The memory of Prussia's feudal dependence on Poland was later systematically eliminated from historical accounts. King Frederick William I attempted to have all books referring to it burned, and threatened anyone who mentioned it with severe punishment.

Frederick's coronation was also opposed by the Papacy. Despite interventions by influential Catholics in Prussian pay, Rome had not recognised the 1525 secularisation and still refused to acknowledge Hohenzollern rule over Prussia. Although hostile papal treatises could not stop the coronation, Catholic Europe was generally slow to recognise it [219; 63–82].

The Königsberg ceremonies were a masterpiece of sophisticated stage-management. The self-coronation – following the example of Charles XII of Sweden in 1697 – emphasised that it was not God, but the monarch's human agency that created power in the world, as von Besser observed: 'His Majesty received his realm not from the estates or any other assistance, but according to the example of the most ancient kings by his own doing ... For he already possessed all of the regalia by virtue of his sovereignty' [222; 15–16]. By inaugurating the ceremonial Order of the Black Eagle, the king extended the glory of his new title to his most deserving relatives and courtiers [256; 205]. The estates, however, were treated with manifest disrespect, informed about the ceremony at the last minute and only allowed to watch from a distance.

Handbooks of ceremonial etiquette spoke of monarchical status as 'a superiority which turns into law ... a title of prerogative or precedence' [218; 101–13]. This was echoed in French writings on absolute rulership, such as Jacques Bossuet's definition of monarchy as a combination of sacrality, paternalism, absolute power and reason [99; 57–9]. In contrast to medieval ideas of divine right monarchy, sanctioned by spiritual power and the Roman Church, Frederick's master-of-ceremonies characterised Prussian sovereignty in highly personal terms: 'From Frederick the Third thou now becomest the First, for thou art the first to invent thy Crown. ... All royal power and sovereignty already belonged to him, and his coronation and enthronement could be none other than what he performed upon himself and his consort' [222; 16]. Yet this projection of royal authority could only have any impact if other European rulers and the king's own subjects recognised its legitimacy.

Christian Wolff, the renowned Prussian philosopher, clearly perceived the importance of rituals for legitimacy, admitting that 'the common man cannot grasp the nature of kingship, but through things which touch his senses, especially eyesight, he attains a vague idea of its power. This shows that a luxurious court and its ceremonies are far from superfluous or worthy of reproach' [352; 466]. Andreas Gestrich's research on the relationship between absolutism and the public sphere confirms Wolff's observation that public acceptance of rulership could not simply be enforced by decree from above, but was dependent on communication [228].

For this dialogue with the public Frederick could not entirely dispense with religious symbolism. Calvinists, Lutherans, and a new movement, the Pietists, who called for a continued reformation through the promotion of greater godliness in society (see Chapter 6), struggled for influence over the coronation. Despite Friedrich's conscious distance from all denominations, he knew that a coronation without anointment was less than respectable, particularly in the eyes of Catholic rulers. Anointment could only be performed by a bishop, an office assumed by the territorial rulers after 1544. Consequently, in his role as highest patron of his churches, Frederick created two bishops, nominating a Calvinist and a Lutheran theologian to officiate. He prescribed for sermons across his realm Psalm 89:20–1: King David's anointment as God's servant. The symbolic humility in the sermons' emphasis on the monarch's role as guardian of the people was designed to win public support for the legitimacy of the new monarchy by stressing its religious foundation. As one of Frederick's advisors argued, the anointment would demonstrate that the Prussian monarchy – in contrast to its former Polish suzerain – was based on divine sanction, not a contract with the people [219; 21–41].

[ii] The Polycentric Kingdom

The communication of power through the medium of ceremonies is just one theme of the new cultural history of politics. The location of power in the court and the ruler's residences constitute another. The highly specific court culture of the Hohenzollern monarchy was shaped by the fact that its territories were widely scattered. There was no capital city comparable to Vienna, London or Paris, but a polycentric arrangement of residences and administrative centres. The Brandenburg court had originated in the southern territories of the Franconian line, in Ansbach and Bayreuth, whose administrative personnel contributed to the staffing of new Hohenzollern courts. In Prussia, Duke Albrecht of Hohenzollern-Ansbach composed his first Court Ordinance in 1564 for his Franconian officials at Königsberg castle. As such rule books became more detailed, they played an increasing role as instruments of social and confessional disciplining [231].

Elector Joachim II, at the very start of his Brandenburg reign in 1535, started constructing an electoral castle in Cölln on the River Spree to provide a residential centre, falling into heavy debt in the process. The expansion of residences with representational purposes and for hunting expeditions between Berlin, Cölln and Potsdam, shows the close connection and permeability between political and private residential functions. When Brandenburg and Prussia were joined permanently under John Sigismund, the considerable distances between his territories constituted a considerable challenge for the establishment of a court culture predicated upon the ruler's personal presence [243].

The centre of power shifted as the prince moved around, while local governors, chambers, consistories, councils and colleges stepped into the void to uphold authority, often requiring support from the provincial estates. The scattered Hohenzollern residences served as transitory accommodation for peripatetic rulers trying to hold their composite state together. Thus as Frederick William sought after 1648 to consolidate his administrative institutions in Berlin-Cölln, where the estate assemblies of Brandenburg gathered and swore homage, the central law court met and the consistory, the chancellery and the privy council were established, he was distracted by the need to appear in his newly-acquired territory of Cleves, far away on the Rhine.

During most of Frederick William's reign Königsberg castle outshone its counterpart in Berlin [218; 73–89]. After 1680, the aging Elector finally instigated a comprehensive programme of civil architecture for his residences in Potsdam, Schwedt, Köpenick and Berlin. The desire to improve his lacklustre residences compelled the Baroque monarch Frederick I to call two famous architects and sculptors to Berlin: Eosander von Göthe and, from 1694, Andreas Schlüter, who had previously worked in Warsaw. From 1692, Frederick had extended Oranienburg to honour his family's Dutch heritage and the house of Orange. He dedicated the castle Lietzenburg to his second wife Sophie Charlotte of Hanover; renamed Charlottenburg after her death, it became the king's main summer residence [248; 59–74].

This expansion was accompanied by the proliferation of court offices. In 1691 the court table of precedence contained 34 ranks; in 1705 the number had grown to 131 [227; 53–87]. Residential splendour had become a matter of reason of state: Frederick I insisted that he had renovated Berlin castle not for 'pleasure but necessity' [220; 27]. As a regular visitor to the courts of London, Berlin and Hanover, when the British political agent and writer John Toland praised the Prussian militia and focused on the representative qualities of the princely residence in Berlin, 'the finery of their habits and ... the expensiveness of public festivals', he knew what he was talking about [254; 36]. The restoration of Berlin castle was closely connected to the coronation project: between 1698, when planning began, and 1706, the building was fundamentally transformed. Yet, Versailles was never a model for the Hohenzollerns as historians once assumed; Swedish representational architecture and Stockholm castle were far more influential [209; 35].

As in Sweden, the growth of the court challenged the nobility's traditional role. Frederick expanded his residential portfolio, using his feudal prerogatives to coerce noble families into selling their houses, particularly targeting families with a long genealogy who dared to own opulent hunting and summer residences. In contrast to the 1680/82 Swedish *Reduktion*, which returned alienated royal domains to the monarch, Frederick's strategy of requisitioning noble properties came at a considerable price. He bought over 50 noble villages, including the Altlandsberg domains of Otto von Schwerin, Frederick William's loyal minister, whose grandson was forced in 1705 to give up his family residence. Between 1691 and 1711 Frederick acquired no fewer than eight noble seats which joined newly-built summer and hunting castles in a ring of fourteen new and renovated establishments around Berlin. Nearby court employees and their families were settled whose opulent houses increasingly encroached upon the old civic structures of towns such as Potsdam and Berlin-Cölln and contrasted starkly with the simpler urban architecture [218].

[iii] The Court and Eighteenth-century Monarchy

Historians from the late eighteenth century onward have praised Frederick William I's rule as a model of rationality that set Prussia on the road to great power status. His accession had dramatic consequences for Berlin's economy and life at the court. The new king sacked most of the craftsmen and architects in the royal household, dissolved the Swiss guard, shrunk the number of ranks to 47, slashed salaries in half and radically reduced expenses to almost an eighth of their previous level. He sacked the court orchestra, sent the horses from the royal stables to the cavalry and sold the porcelain collection to Saxony, all because of the 'great debt of the country, an empty treasury and the great oppression of the citizens by all kinds of duties', as Friedrich Nicolai complained in his *Description of the Royal Residential Cities Berlin and Potsdam*. Mass bankruptcies ensued, and Berlin's population stagnated at around 60,000 – having tripled between 1680 and 1709 [209, 211; I/lvii]. While craft guilds had experienced a golden age under his father, Frederick William made Brandenburg the only territory in the Empire where an imperial law against abusive craft practices was enforced in separate regulations in 1734 and 1736, radically reducing the guilds' legal and economic autonomies [213; 114]. Whether Frederick William's sudden disinvestment was a wise move, is still controversial. He certainly did not share his father's policy of letting 'the money roll about in his own country, so that the subjects could live' [229; 35].

Frederick William did not completely renounce all representation, however. He invested large sums into his *Lange Kerle*, particularly tall soldiers collected from across Europe to fill the ranks of his Lifeguards, while the gardens were converted into a drill ground for his troops [226]. He introduced quirky amusements to court life, such as the Tobacco College, his favourite male circle which combined excessive smoking and drinking with mocking the 'court fool' and president of the Berlin Academy of Sciences, Jacob Paul Gundling [338; 198–218]. Such rough entertainment contrasted notably with the refinement of Frederick I's Baroque court and Sophie Charlotte's libraries. How could this new court maintain his claim to legitimacy among European styles of representation? Benjamin Marschke, challenging traditional historiography which simply believed the soldier king's assertion that his authority was like a 'rock of bronze', presents much evidence of Frederick William's insecurity as his fellow monarchs proved slow to receive Prussia into their circle [164]. The king resorted to a policy of 'occasional pomp and circumstance'. His tendency to economise should not be exaggerated: for representational reasons the expansion of Berlin Castle continued unabated, royal weddings were celebrated in accustomed style, and the queen maintained a lavish court at Monbijou, while diplomats were impressed by the ceremonial. Frederick William I's abandonment of his father's Baroque style coincided with the end of the age of Louis XIV. Precedence rituals had become cumbersome to many European courts. Yet in the same way that favours or snubs given to competing nobles in Versailles had become part of court life, the soldier king's informal demeanour and his conspicuous frugality played an intended role in the courtly representational game of 'anti-ceremonial ceremony' [164; 243].

More important than the abandoning of opulence, however, were the changes introduced to the exercise of power and patronage which had bound courtiers, government and crown in Berlin together. The king's style of government foreshadowed his successor's in one respect: he ruled from Wusterhausen and Potsdam, taking decisions among his advisors, in his cabinet, or alone, while central administrative institutions remained in Berlin [248; 75–88]. The separation between the king and his cabinet in Potsdam on the one hand, and the governmental institutions in Berlin on the other, became permanent.

After the 1740 conquest of Silesia, Frederick II declared Potsdam 'as much His [Majesty's] residence as Berlin' [210; 273–96]. Royal government was now supported by highly valued cabinet secretaries, some of non-noble background, occasionally with university education [83]. The administrative apparatus in Berlin, however, whose size should not be overestimated, remained firmly in noble hands. Its role was boosted by the centralising reforms introduced in the early 1720s. The king's absence from the court also changed its character: courtiers were increasingly replaced by military and administrative officers. Neugebauer speaks of a partial privatisation, Chris Clark of a partial militarisation and masculinisation of the courtly sphere in Berlin, where public drill exercises replaced artistic spectacles [210, 13; 34].

Frederick II continued the depoliticisation of court culture, investing generously in the artistic and representational functions of Berlin. Petitions to the queen or the princes were a waste of time as they had no influence over the king. At the same time, the king authorised private secretaries to conduct diplomatic meetings without the knowledge of relevant ministers. Frederick II negotiated with individual departments rather than through the civil service of the General Directory, which he gave a less collegial shape [74; 19–29]. This undermined the authority of central institutions and asserted the personal power of the king and his immediate advisers, who usually met in his private rooms. The extent to which this endangered governmental efficiency and cohesion became evident after 1786, when the less forceful Frederick William II succeeded his uncle. The character of absolute monarchy as a personal pursuit, above and beyond clearly regulated bureaucratic channels, gave an additional meaning to the motto of the 'first servant of the state': the king as 'private man' was always also the politician, constantly shadowed by his secretaries and attendants. The personal cabinet was no advance over older structures, since it confused ordered layers of responsibility and competence. Frederick II's regime cannot be credited with the invention of the modern bureaucratic state.

[iv] Military Monarchy and the Cities

While the building of the court in and around Berlin launched the city's rise as a cultural and economic centre, its eighteenth-century growth into a major capital has often been credited to the monarchy's mercantilism and the presence of a growing commercial elite which profited from the needs of the military state. The impact of large garrisons and the investment in the army, however, has become a matter of controversy as scholars assess the modernising impact of the military on Brandenburg-Prussian cities rather more critically. The core provinces of Brandenburg, Ducal Prussia and Pomerania were not famed for their robust urban culture. Over half of all Brandenburg urban dwellers in 1773 lived in five cities, with the overwhelming majority located in Berlin [207]. Nineteenth-century liberals saw urban populations as allies in their attempt to revive self-government and initiate social reform in Prussia. If Schmoller considered the cities as the main forum for rulers' progressive central reforms, hampered by urban magistrates opposed to change [212], Carsten gloomily describes the decline of Prussia's cities, brought down by an unholy alliance of a powerful nobility and its imposing rulers [2; 136–48]. This approach suited the paradigm of the Prussian *Sonderweg*. Büsch reinforced this picture when he blamed the slow development of a self-confident Prussian bourgeoisie on the militarisation of society and its will to imitate aristocracy [296].

In contrast to the commercial patriciate of Polish Prussia's largest cities Danzig, Thorn and Elbing – which maintained seats in the Polish Prussian regional Diet, and whose trade by far surpassed that of Brandenburg-Prussia before the first partition of Poland isolated them from their economic hinterlands in 1772 – many of Brandenburg-Prussia's cities were transformed into garrisons during the first half of the eighteenth century. They had already lost most of their autonomy to appointed royal tax commissars, often posted from other territories of the monarchy, who collected contributions with little local knowledge or compassion. Frederick William I subordinated the administration of the urban excise tax to the General War Commissariat whose officials increasingly interfered with local government [215]. Most cities had no judicial autonomy, not even in minor matters. After Frederick William's 1722/3 reforms, urban society was closely subject to central restrictions on new buildings and on migration, which reduced opportunities to expand and, perhaps more importantly, to build a sense of civic identity and communal autonomy [204].

Traditionally at the crossroads of Central European trade, Breslau – after its occupation by Prussia in 1740 – had been separated from its commercial networks and visibly deteriorated. It lost its armouries and salt stocks and was burdened with high taxation, which was not reinvested in times of need, such as the Seven Years War [217]. In garrisoned cities, during conflicts between the military and civilian population, the military turned rapidly to their own personnel and judges, who found themselves in greater favour with the monarch than civil magistrates. The councillors of Königsberg complained in 1719 that soldiers stationed in the city 'mingle too often in civil matters of no concern to them, which depresses the dispositions and corrupts trade and our way of life' [212; 572]. The sheer numbers seem to confirm this picture: in Potsdam in 1780 a civilian population of around 19,000 hosted 8000 members of the armed forces [299].

Since the Great Elector's draconian actions against Königsberg in the 1660s and again in 1673–4, when he bullied the city with the threat of military execution into accepting restrictions on its autonomy, the political influence of the cities had been curtailed. In contrast, even the smaller towns in Polish Prussia – politically active, albeit economically declining – managed to build urban alliances among themselves to represent their interests against an overbearing nobility: first in 1683, then again in 1702 and 1738 [202].

Blickle has argued that rural and urban subjects shared a sense of 'communalism', which strengthened their identity in defence of local immunities and participation [203]. There is, however, little evidence of such communalism in the towns of Brandenburg-Prussia, where the double domination of noble owners and the demands of the central treasury diminished economic and political spaces for manoeuvre [203; 333–58]. From 1749, cities could no longer sell or lease landed properties, and in 1766 the General Directory assumed exclusive control over their budgets. Four years later, urban jurisdiction was seriously curtailed. Breslau, despite its great commercial tradition, did not have a single merchant in its council chamber between 1740 and 1793.

Under Frederick II, the introduction of the French tax regime under the name of *Régie* further undermined the opportunity of urban crafts to recover their productivity. There is evidence that merchants avoided towns where heavy contributions in the form of the excise were levied. State monopolies, supported by the *Régie*, destroyed what was left of local guilds. Finally, even ministers lost faith in such policies: in 1794, the Silesian minister Count Hoym wrote that 'in this province the taxes on beer, spirits and meat resulted in such economic decline that some places already have not a single brewery or butcher left' [217; 42]. Imitating the Russian minister Potemkin, the Prussian tax commissaries ordered local craftsmen to simulate building work during Frederick's visit to Silesia to obscure the penury in which they lived [319]. Not all territories accepted interference without a struggle: the Westphalian manufacturing cities successfully lobbied against burdensome Kanton obligations, and after 1763 achieved the exemption of a whole district including major factory cities [300; 167–90].

Recent historiography has tried to adjust this negative picture. Research on the socio-economic conditions of garrison cities has demonstrated that in some cases the military contributed to urban prosperity and security, which provided compensation for lost autonomies [208]. The quartering of troops in civilian houses burdened the urban population considerably, but it was also a source of income, reflected in a growing market for rented accommodation. The demand for manufactured goods, such as armaments, uniforms, craft products and victuals invigorated commerce and production. Garrison cities played an increasingly significant role in the national economy. Most importantly, soldiers – often from a rural background – adopted urban habits and manners. While the smoking of tobacco under Frederick William I was still an elite pursuit, by the end of the eighteenth century it had been spread widely by soldiers returning home to their villages after their Kanton service. In some cases, such cohabitation led to the 'urbanisation' of the military, not the militarisation of civil society [299].

The government benefited most from quartering men in cities, as such practices prevented high desertion rates and imposed stricter controls on the behaviour of soldiers and urban inhabitants alike. A large volume of decrees began to regulate civilian-military relations during the second half of the seventeenth century during the construction of what Marc Raeff called the 'well-ordered police state' [89], although most people were aware of the gap between legal theory and practice. The symbiosis of military and urban interests embraced the most intimate spheres: marriages to local women, socialising in local pubs, and the choice of soldiers as godparents by urban families demonstrates that a peaceful and harmonious coexistence was possible. This symbiosis furthered social mobility by soldiers who, after their departure from the army, often returned to the city in which they had been stationed and became honoured citizens of the town [300; 191–217].

The treatment of Polish Prussian and Polish cities, occupied by hostile Prussian armies during the three partitions of Poland in 1772, 1793 and 1795, differed considerably, however [21]. Breslau also experienced a rougher treatment until the end of Frederick II's reign, when it slowly recovered its economic strength to become Prussia's third residential city after Berlin and Potsdam. In 1752, Frederick II decided that Prussian cities deserved protection from overzealous military occupation. The decree that 'no military commander can usurp authority over the magistracy and townsmen' did not mean the end of military jurisdiction over civic matters, but the introduction of mixed (civil-military) courts [74; 67–8]. Free elections of the magistrates only persisted in Magdeburg and in the western provinces such as Cleves. Cities that had suffered most, such as Breslau or Danzig, eventually turned into some of the most enthusiastic supporters of the Prussian war effort against Napoleon [318]. An emerging sense of a Prussian urban patriotism can be gleaned from the chronicles of master baker Johann Heyde in Berlin, who closely followed news of the Seven Years War and their diplomatic ramifications [214].

For foreign travellers, Berlin symbolised the new Prussian military monarchy which had taken on much of Europe during the Seven Years War and survived. This image, later expanded by Thomas Carlyle with a mixture of admiration and liberal criticism, was confirmed by other British observers such as Neville Wyndham, who wrote in 1790 during a visit to Berlin: 'There is no town in Europe, not even Constantinople, which has so large a garrison.' The implications of this comparison with a despotic regime seem clear. But it was not only Frederick II's unscrupulous policies that propelled the provincial capital of Brandenburg into the European limelight. Around 1790, when Wyndham visited, Berlin had 150,000 inhabitants and had become a bustling city of salons and Enlightenment culture. The monarchy had started its life in Königsberg, which maintained its provincial character despite Immanuel Kant's role at its university. The eighteenth-century ideals of merit, professionalisation and education had their subversive effects on the aristocratic milieu of the military establishment and sparked what Holger Gräf has called the 'enlightenment of the military', which peaked with the military reforms of Gerhard von Scharnhorst and August von Gneisenau in the early years of the nineteenth century [299; 103]. Again, revision should not go too far. Whenever Prussia's military monarchs clashed with traditions of civic autonomy, the values of civility and urbanity were on the defensive. Despite many visits to the enlightened salons of Berlin and Breslau, military officers never quite became citizen soldiers – they remained their king's most loyal servants.

5 Foreign Policies between East and West

For nineteenth-century historians who believed in the primacy of foreign policy, the story of Prussia was dominated by its role in the unification of Germany between 1867 and 1871. Earlier periods served as the pre-history to this event [71]. This changed in the 1960s, when social history became the dominant paradigm. The primacy of foreign policy underwent a much contested revival as a 'revisionist approach' in the works of Anglo-Saxon historians of Prussia such as Brendan Simms, Tim Blanning, Derek McKay and Hamish M. Scott [287]. These supporters of a fresh approach to foreign policy, however, do not aim to resurrect Borussian hagiography. Instead they link the importance of foreign policy with the security problems that confronted early modern composite states and their rulers when trying to consolidate their widely scattered territories [13; 36–57, 70; 9–32, 280].

The central importance of foreign affairs for absolute monarchy is undeniable, particularly for the reign of Frederick II, who did so much to extend Prussia's borders. Most work on this subject, however, is still done from a Germano-centric or West European perspective. Yet the roles of Prussia's once powerful neighbours, Poland-Lithuania and Sweden, and the north-east European context are vital to the long-term understanding of Brandenburg-Prussian security concerns. This is especially true for the period before 1740, when the Hohenzollern dynasty ruled over a middling electorate within the Empire and was not much more than an auxiliary power in the north-east European theatre of war, dominated by the struggle for control of the Baltic Sea.

Nothing more ambitious should be written back into Brandenburg-Prussia's history before the mid-eighteenth century. The myth of the Great Elector, for example, which still influences textbooks on Prussian history, has to be treated with caution. [92] Frederick William was, like all electoral princes, relatively small fry in the larger European picture. His achievements should be compared to those of his main Protestant rivals in the Empire, the Saxon Wettins, and the ambitious Guelphs in Hanover [267, 283]. Even after the conquest of Silesia and parts of Saxony and Polish Prussia, which led to Prussia's later claim to membership in a dominant pentarchy with Britain, Russia, France and Austria, Brandenburg-Prussia's structural weakness as a composite state persisted and was fully exposed in the wars against Napoleonic France. Through several case studies, this chapter charts the limitations and opportunities of Brandenburg-Prussia's foreign policy, from the Reformation to the end of the eighteenth century, in its double orientation towards East and West which was marked by the eclipse of the three powers that had defined Prussia's polices for so long: Poland-Lithuania, Sweden and the Holy Roman Empire.

[i] Imperial Limitations: Brandenburg-Prussia in the Seventeenth Century

After the upheavals of the early Reformation, the Peace of Augsburg of 1555 had established a *modus vivendi* in the Empire. Brandenburg and Electoral Saxony took the lead in trying to reconcile 'princely liberality' and confessional freedom with loyalty towards the Empire and the Emperor [10; 162 ff.] .The greatest weakness of the Augsburg settlement was the exclusion of the Calvinists, who continued working for its revision. This, together with the Catholic counter-attack and the imperial constitutional and legal crisis, pitted Catholic and Protestant claims against each other and eventually led to the Thirty Years War.

Lutheran Electoral Saxony had emerged as the leader of the Protestants in the Empire, despite its hostility towards Calvinism, the religion of the Hohenzollern dynasty. The Swedish invasion of the Empire in 1630 made Brandenburg's position even more difficult. Instead of relieving Magdeburg, which was destroyed by Catholic troops in 1631, the Swedes marched on Berlin, compelling George William to abandon the pro-Habsburg line of his controversial Catholic minister Adam von Schwarzenberg, and hesitantly join the Swedes. In 1632 the Swedes occupied and plundered Bavaria, but Albrecht von Wallenstein, commander of the Habsburg armies, stemmed the tide, particularly after Gustav Adolf's death at the battle of Lützen in the same year. Swedish intervention had nevertheless changed the course of the war, and the Protestant princes continued to expand their influence in the Empire.

Dependence on Sweden was difficult for George William, who had the strongest claim to succeed the last childless duke in Pomerania, Bogislav XIV, who died in 1634. In 1630 Gustav Adolf had claimed the Pomeranian duchy as compensation for Swedish involvement in the war. This dispute sent Brandenburg back into a reluctant alliance with the Emperor. Brandenburg's reputation benefited from its participation as one of the four army contingents (next to Saxony, Austria and Bavaria) set up in the 1635 Peace of Prague for the defence of the Empire. In the context of the pro-imperial patriotism that accompanied these peace negotiations, initiated by Saxony and subsequently accepted by most Protestant princes, the Pomeranian political writer Bogislav Philipp von Chemnitz warned the princes against the Habsburg 'tyrant' and demanded the Emperor's subordination to the Imperial Diet and the law [271]. Despite its cooperation with the Empire, Brandenburg shared this view: being pro-imperial (*reichisch*) was not the same as supporting the Emperor's political goals (*kaiserlich*).

When in 1640 Frederick William succeeded to the electoral title, his task looked daunting. The Swedes had occupied two-thirds of Brandenburg and were drawing substantial contributions from it to help fund their massive war effort. From 1643, the Elector tried to improve his position by negotiating with France, which in turn humiliated him, forcing him to call the very young Louis XIV 'majesty', instead of 'brother' – the title European rulers used for those of equal status [253]. The 'beggarly elector' had to make peace [239]. He even toyed with the idea of marrying Christina of Sweden to solve his territorial claims to Pomerania and end the Swedish occupation, but she was unimpressed. The Elector turned his father's pro-imperial legacy on its head and reinstated pro-Swedish councillors, supported by the estates, who had resented Schwarzenberg's absolutist style. By signing a truce with the Swedes which lasted until 1648 but gave him no advantages, the Elector recognised that his options were limited. Residing in Königsberg, he kept a safe distance from the war that devastated most of his Brandenburg lands. The Electorate, on which his status in the Empire depended, was a token held by foreigners in the intricate game of poker that lead up to the Peace of Westphalia.

After 1648 Frederick William enacted reforms to build a standing army, but was only marginally more successful than his rivals. The peace negotiations did not win him half of his demands (see Chapter 3). The possibilities open to Frederick William were limited not merely by his poor military and financial resources, but more importantly by the political reforms in the Empire, which protected the smaller states against the larger and more aggressive ones. What he could achieve was heavily circumscribed by imperial law and institutions and by the electorate's very position as a guarantor of that system. The laws of the Empire secured the position of the Emperor, who, as most imperial princes agreed even if reluctantly, had to come from a dynastic house with the resources and the prestige of the Habsburgs [267; 33–64]. By building on the work of Karl Otmar von Aretin, Press and other German historians who in the 1980s began to challenge the negative Prusso-German view of the Empire which pervaded most older historiography, Wilson has demonstrated the Empire's resilience in the late seventeenth and eighteenth centuries [18, 291]. Brandenburg's critical distance to the Empire was still obvious in the Elector's distaste for the closely binding confessional and political alliance networks which most middling and smaller territories sought in the post-1648 Empire. Frederick William thought them too restrictive and instead initiated a political course of bilateral treaties and pacts which were easier to renounce [9; 43].

Historians traditionally attributed this preference to the Elector's unashamedly self-interested *Fuchspolitik* ('politics of a fox'), which gave him the reputation of being unreliable. It is certainly true that his course changed as frequently as his alliances, having vowed, in contrast to his father's unsuccessful policy of neutrality, 'never to be neutral again till I die' [239; 210]. In his testament he pressed home this point, warning his successor 'that your land, if you sit still and think that the fire is far from your borders ..., will be the main stage for tragedy' [70; 13]. Such pragmatism, however, was tempered by the Elector's religious motivation, which strongly influenced his foreign policy. He continued, for example, to support the Dutch Republic, despite its repeated refusal to trust or help him: 'religion is the chief reason for not wanting to see the States [General of the Netherlands] destroyed; they are surrounded by Catholics; neutrality would make us a worm which lets itself be eaten' [239; 201].

Another reason for his constant change of allies was his search for subsidies to maintain the growing number of his troops, which he needed to create respect and status. The clever exploitation of the imperial defence system, particularly after 1681, when cash allocations from imperial princes unable to muster large defence forces benefited Brandenburg, sustaining the continuous build-up of the Hohenzollern armies, but did not sufficiently address the Elector's security concerns (see Chapter 2). After a series of treaties concluded and broken with France, whose hegemonic protection the Elector never desired but was usually forced to accept, he built his military reputation at Fehrbellin in 1675. After a long series of military failures, it was the first time that Brandenburg troops had defeated the Swedes unaided; the fact that it was almost twice as large as the Elector's force merely increased Fehrbellin's propaganda value. Although his troops subsequently occupied the whole of Pomerania, Frederick William could not press home his victory: the Franco-Swedish alliance once more denied him this prize during the 1679 Nijmegen peace negotiations. He finally turned his back on France in 1686, after the Revocation of the Edict of Nantes exiled almost 40,000 French Huguenots, many of whom were welcomed in Brandenburg (see Chapter 2).

The Great Elector never achieved the position in international relations he craved, for all his military success and his personal connection to the Dutch through his first wife Luise Henriette. He remained the prince of a subsidiary state that could supply auxiliary – albeit well-trained – troops, led by talented commanders. He had not won the trust of greater powers. It was only when the army could be supported from Brandenburg-Prussia's own resources that the strategy of 'necessity' could become a long-term policy of 'reason of state' [70; 30].

When considering Frederick William's vacillating foreign policy, it is easy to forget that after 1648 it became easier for Brandenburg to be pro-imperial, since Calvinism had been recognised as one of the official confessions of the Empire. In return, toleration for Catholics under Hohenzollern rule was necessary because of Brandenburg-Prussia's recognition of imperial laws. The Elector's unwillingness to burn bridges to the Emperor was reflected in his reluctance to become a French client in the League of the Rhine, which he only joined in 1665 when it was breaking up. On the whole, indeed, Frederick William proved a conservative pillar of the imperial hierarchy, defending the pre-eminence of the Electoral College after

1648, against the challenge of a rival alliance of non-electoral princes. In return, he received the other electors' support for his advocacy of paragraph 180 of the Imperial Recess in 1654, which granted the princes the right to demand that defence costs be met by their territorial estates [69].

Yet if the Recess increased the Hohenzollern rulers' authority over their imperial territories, most other features of the Empire limited it. One of these was imperial jurisprudence. The Supreme Imperial Court showed a keen interest in Brandenburg affairs. Even in 1806 imperial jurisdiction still applied to all imperial lands under Hohenzollern rule, or 53 per cent of Brandenburg-Prussia's population [291]. The 1750 privilege of no appeal granted to Frederick II prevented subjects from presenting local cases to the imperial courts, but this did not apply to cases involving matters outside the Hohenzollern realm. The privilege also did not stop prosecution of Hohenzollern subjects and lands by other imperial princes for breach of imperial law.

In Brandenburg, the main centre of legal learning was the university of Halle, founded in 1694, where future officials studied imperial constitutional law in preparation for their professional life. Officials posted to the western territories under Hohenzollern rule were more directly exposed to imperial politics than their counterparts east of the Elbe. Frederick III/I and Frederick William I both worked within the imperial context and continued a pro-imperial course. In return, Brandenburg continued to contribute to the cohesion of the Empire and its institutions such as the Upper Saxon circle, which sent delegates to the imperial supreme court in Speyer and, from 1693, in Wetzlar. Prussian–Austrian dualism does not have the long history Borussian writers gave it in the nineteenth century: it was created virtually overnight by Frederick II's illegal invasion and annexation of Silesia, an act that challenged imperial tradition and overturned the whole tradition of Hohenzollern imperial policy.

[ii] The Rise of Prussia in North-east Europe

As electors of Brandenburg the Hohenzollern princes had to deal with the emperor's power in Germany. As dukes of Prussia, they had to reckon with the king of Poland and the Polish-Lithuanian Commonwealth. These factors imposed limitations of a different kind, but also, in the seventeenth century, provided important opportunities that were ultimately to transform the position of the Hohenzollern dynastic agglomeration. Initially, the 1525 treaty with Poland provided Duke Albrecht of Hohenzollern with vital protection against the anger of Emperor Charles V over the secularisation of the Teutonic Order. In constant fear of reprisals from the Emperor and the Pope, Albrecht remained a loyal vassal of the Polish crown. As the powerful Catholic clergy opposed the integration of Prussia's Protestant population which would have weakened the Catholic position in the Polish crown lands, Albrecht rested assured that Poland had no designs to incorporate the duchy. At the same time, Albrecht's knowledge of Poland and its culture made him a useful partner. The duke's support for Polish Lutheran education and clerical training, particularly at the newly-founded University of Königsberg (1544), flew in the face of the imperial and papal ban imposed on the duchy's institutions [206]. For the Protestants in Poland-Lithuania, the duchy of Prussia was a lifeline for the production and dissemination of printed material.

After Albrecht's death in 1568, the highest councillors assumed government in the duchy on account of the mental illness of his successor, Albert Frederick, until in 1577 the Polish king, Stefan Batory, authorised the Franconian margrave George Frederick of Ansbach and Kulmbach (1577–1603) to govern as curator and co-regent. Astute marriage policies soon connected the two lines more directly. John Sigismund of the Electoral Brandenburg line married Albert Frederick's daughter Anna in 1594. Through her mother she had claims to the two north-western provinces of Jülich-Berg-Ravensberg and Cleves-Mark, whose ruler died in 1609 without leaving a direct heir but several relatives across the Empire who claimed the right of succession. The two main contenders were the Hohenzollerns and the Pfalz-Neuburgs, who divided the inheritance in 1614. With the end of the Ansbach-Kulmbach line – George Frederick died without leaving an heir – the Brandenburg-Prussian marriage ensured that the electoral line also had a tangible dynastic claim to Prussia (see Appendix 2).

As the duchy was still a fief of the Polish crown, Brandenburg electors needed Polish consent to their succession. After 1525 it had been extended in 1563 to the Franconian line; between 1605 and 1618, the Polish king and diet repeatedly confirmed the right of succession to individual rulers of the Brandenburg line. With the death of

Albert Frederick in 1618 the electoral line negotiated a permanent right to succession. This success was partly due to Poland-Lithuania's need for an ally – or at least for Brandenburg's neutrality in its developing conflict with Sweden – but it was also the result of lobbying by the Prussian estates at the Polish Diet in Warsaw. The elector now ruled over extended composite territories bordering powerful states, including Poland-Lithuania, the Netherlands and, from 1648, Swedish Pomerania. Voltaire's bon mot that Prussia was a 'kingdom of border strips', a result of sixteenth-century dynastic coincidence, marriage and inheritance policies, reflected in a nutshell the problems the electors faced. 'Prussia as a united element of action is not more than an abstraction', commented one historian [170]; its relations with its northern and eastern neighbours, Poland-Lithuania and Sweden, certainly bear this out.

Duke Albrecht had conducted an active foreign policy towards the Baltic powers. His plans to secularise the Livonian Order also failed due to the Muscovite invasion of Livonia in 1558. In 1561 Courland (Western Latvia and Semgallia) was secularised instead by the last grand master of the Livonian Order, Gotthard von Kettler, who followed Albrecht's example and turned Courland into a Polish fief. Both of them were sucked into the first of the long series of wars between Muscovy, Denmark, Sweden and Poland-Lithuania that became known as the Northern Wars [298].

Strengthened by the 1569 Union between Lithuania and Poland, which created one parliament and ensured the better coordination of the Polish and Lithuanian armies, the Polish-Lithuanian Commonwealth emerged as the strongest power in north-east Europe. After the death of the last Jagiellonian king, the country adopted the principle of the free election of the monarch in 1573 by the Commonwealth's entire nobility.

In 1587 the Catholic heir to the Swedish throne, Sigismund Vasa, whose mother was Katarzyna Jagiellonka, sister of the last king of the Jagiellonian dynasty, was elected king of Poland. When, after a brief personal union between Poland-Lithuania and Sweden, Sigismund was expelled from Sweden by his Protestant uncle, a period of Polish-Swedish wars erupted which lasted until 1660 and fundamentally changed the relationship between Poland and the Duchy of Prussia.

After military successes in Polish Livonia, the Swedish armies invaded the commonwealth's north-eastern shores in May 1626 and turned on the rich cities of Poland's province of Royal Prussia [298; 102–32]. Sweden was on its journey to great power status. By 1660, Sweden had broken Danish control of the Sound and annexed Denmark's provinces in the southern Scandinavian peninsula. In alliance with France it had diminished Habsburg influence, laid waste to large parts of Germany, and signed the Peace of Westphalia as one of its guarantors. Having gained a foothold on the southern Baltic coast in the rich province of Western Pomerania, Sweden had become Brandenburg's most eminent competitor in the northeast. The mediators, including the elector of Brandenburg, were so worried about Habsburg victories in the Empire that they caved in to Swedish demands. This put considerable strain on the Great Elector's relations with Poland.

Historians of Prussia have largely ignored this context of Frederick William's policies during and after the Thirty Years War. Sweden's success was all the more astonishing, given its meagre demographic and economic resources, and can only be explained by the emergence of the Swedish military state. Based on a political system which included representatives from the free peasantry, Sweden created a service class which supported the expansionist foreign policies of its dynasty in return for land and offices. Waging war in foreign fields was vital; the principle that war must feed war was considered the only possibility for a relatively poor country to provision and maintain its armies. These armies were to a considerable degree composed of natives, in contrast to the mercenary systems which still prevailed in most other contemporary armies. The Swedish model was to be of crucial importance for Brandenburg-Prussia's development, particularly for the emergence of the standing army and the Prussian Kanton system, which drew heavily on the Swedish example [304].

When the Swedes renewed their war against the Commonwealth under Charles X Gustav in 1655, Frederick William understood that the conflict could either spell disaster or win him considerable influence if he played his cards right. He had built up an army of 17,000 by the autumn of 1655. While a Swedish defeat might have brought him the coveted prize of its Pomeranian lands, by December, fortress after fortress had fallen to the Swedes, and the Elector faced a Swedish ultimatum. In January 1656, in breach of the allegiance he owed to Poland, he accepted Swedish overlordship in Ducal Prussia as the price for his military assistance, and

Brandenburg troops played a key role in the Swedish victory at the battle of Warsaw in July. As the Polish revival continued despite this defeat, the Elector won Swedish recognition of his sovereignty over the duchy in November in the treaty of Labiau, which also promised him extensive territorial gains in Great Poland.

The wars of the so-called Swedish Deluge were a major turning point for the fortunes of the Polish-Lithuanian Commonwealth. Fighting a rebellion of the Zaporozhian Cossacks, who after 1654 joined a Muscovite attack on its eastern border, and facing Swedish and Brandenburg armies in the north, the Commonwealth realised that this was a war for survival [297]. Victory could only come with foreign assistance. The Austrian Habsburgs joined the war on Poland's side, but in the tense political situation in the Empire after Westphalia they were keen to reach a settlement. Frederick William was therefore able to demand a high price: the recognition of Hohenzollern sovereignty over Ducal Prussia, the Royal Prussian city of Elbing and smaller dominions near the Polish-Pomeranian border.

Polish historians have seen the treaties of Wehlau and Bromberg of 1657 as the first step towards the eighteenth-century partitions of Poland. Yet the treaty was sensible given the hard choices the Commonwealth faced: no territory was permanently ceded, and its negotiation left Poland room for manoeuvre in the future [265; 297; 100–5]. Indeed, Elbing was recovered in 1660, and the duchy would return to Polish rule if the Hohenzollerns should die out in the male line. The fact that Poland was never subsequently in a position to reverse its terms had everything to do with a new series of debilitating wars in which Brandenburg-Prussia took little or no part. The claim that, on account of Wehlau-Bromberg, 'Brandenburg-Prussia took the place previously held by Poland-Lithuania in European affairs', is unconvincing [268; 3–4]. Such a perspective overestimates Frederick William's own freedom of manoeuvre. The major change in the balance of power in Europe was the result not of the treaties of Wehlau and Bromberg, but of the expansion of Russia in the early eighteenth century as a consequence of its crushing victory over Sweden in the Great Northern War (1700–21).

Following the defeat at Poltava in 1709 against a reformed Russian army under Peter I (r. 1682–1725), the Swedes under Charles XII lost their great power status and most of their gains on the continent. After a massive mobilisation of troops in 1715, this time without foreign assistance, Frederick William I finally succeeded in occupying the West Pomeranian territories, which improved Prussia's access to the Baltic and allowed the king to continue his comprehensive internal reforms to consolidate his territories.

The consequences of the Swedish retreat from its continental positions before and after 1718, the year of Charles XII's death, were dramatic. Since the 1650s, Russia had expanded into Poland-Lithuania's eastern borderlands, taking Smolensk, Kiev and the left bank of the River Dnieper at the 1667 truce of Andrusovo, which was confirmed in 1686. With the progressive eclipse of Swedish and Polish power, Russia was increasingly successful in using its vast resources to dominate north-east Europe and the southern Baltic.

Russia exposed Polish military and political impotence by breaking its promise to evacuate Russian troops from the Commonwealth. Peter's intervention in the civil war between the Polish king and a large group of noble rebels resulted in an uneasy peace, which in 1717 limited the army to 24,000 men. The Commonwealth was in disarray, even being denied a role at the Swedish–Russian peace negotiations of 1719–21 [273]. Even before the Great Northern War was over, Frederick William signed the Treaty of Potsdam (1719) with Peter I of Russia, blocking any constitutional changes that could have strengthened Poland-Lithuania militarily or politically. Worried about Russia's rapid rise in the Baltic and its attempt to establish itself as the central trading power on the European continent, Britain mediated a Prussian-Swedish peace treaty in 1720 and supported Hohenzollern interests in Pomerania. This finally allowed Frederick William I to purchase Western Pomerania, Stettin, Usedom and Wollin, although Rügen and territories north of the River Peene remained with Sweden.

A new constellation had formed in north-east Europe. The alliance of the 'three black eagles' (Russia, Prussia and Austria) led to the peace treaty of Nystad in September 1721, which granted Russia extensive Swedish possessions, including Livonia. Russian power had for the first time reached Northern Germany. Its alliances with North German powers, in particular with Prussia, introduced the negative strategies against Poland which characterised Russian–German cooperation until the First World War [293].

German historians have tended to ascribe Prussia's eighteenth-century rise to the genius of its kings and to internal factors, such as centralisation, taxation and the army [84]. The military and diplomatic background of the first two decades of the eighteenth century, however, demonstrates the significance of the north-eastern dimension for the transformation of Prussia's international position. Although the Treaty of Nystad defined Poland-Lithuania as Russia's zone of influence, Prussia was not going to be relegated to the sidelines.

[iii]   Prussia's Greatest King?

In 1772 after the first partition of Poland-Lithuania, a puzzled observer noted in the London Annual Register:

> The invasion of an insignificant province would some years ago have armed half of Europe, and called forth all the attention of the other. We now hold the destruction of a great kingdom, with the consequent disarrangement of power, dominion and commerce, with as total an indifference und unconcern as we could read an account of the extermination of one horde of Tatars by another in the days of Tamerlane.

The partition represented a seismic shift in political morality, 'the first very great breach in the modern political system of Europe', as British observers called it [294; 10–11]. The 'fundamental law' guiding Prussia was no longer the dynastic principle, but expansion 'as much as her power permits' [280; 123]. Frederick II himself admitted that the partition treaty of 1772 was the result of a more cynical approach to power politics, which had begun in 1740 with the unilateral invasion and occupation of Silesia, and the attack on Saxony that triggered the Seven Years War (1756–63). In his own words, deception was a most effective policy: 'to hide one's secret ambition and to appear pacifist until opportunity strikes to apply one's secret virtues' [280; 66]. Internal policies were almost entirely subordinated to the demands of foreign policy, which became the exclusive prerogative of the king.

The unexpected death of Emperor Charles VI in 1740 left a young and inexperienced woman as heir to the throne. Despite the Salic Law that banned Habsburg women from rule, Maria Theresa's right to succeed rested on the Pragmatic Sanction of 1713, a treaty signed by imperial princes to guarantee the indivisibility of the Habsburg territories and the succession of a female ruler in the absence of male heirs. Frederick's actions rendered the Sanction a worthless piece of paper overnight. At a time when power was increasingly quantified in terms of demographic, military and material power, Frederick was keen to test the 75,000- strong army he had inherited, and whose upkeep ate up 70 per cent of annual state income, rising to 87 per cent during the Seven Years War [286; 27]. Exploiting Maria Theresa's manifest weakness, Frederick marched his troops into Silesia. The occupation of this province was also aimed against Saxony, as Silesia separated Saxony from Poland where two Saxon Electors in succession occupied the throne between 1697 and 1763.

In contrast to his father, for whom the imperial institutional and legal system had been sacred, Frederick II displayed open disdain for the Empire. This is reflected in his delegation of imperial relations to a subordinate office, while he conducted other foreign affairs himself [13; 58–84, 83]. Untrained in imperial law, the Prussian king continuously misjudged the importance of imperial institutions for the 'third Germany', the smaller and ecclesiastical territories in the Empire, who saw their interests betrayed by Austria and Prussia alike. While many historians have stressed Frederick's hostility towards the imperial constitution, Wilson has pointed out Frederick's pragmatic approach. As long as it suited him, Frederick promoted the new Wittelsbach Emperor Charles VII (r. 1742–5) against the Habsburgs in exchange for legal prerogatives. He assumed the role of the defender of German liberties against Habsburg despotism by forging anti-Austrian alliances and blocking constitutional reform [291]. As the 'poacher [who] turned gamekeeper' [3; 217], Frederick boosted his legitimacy by inventing a historical tradition of Austro-Prussian dualism that could be re-projected into history to justify Prussia's anti-Habsburg policies. The historiographical acceptance of this picture, first widely disseminated in Frederick's own writings, still influences histories of Germany today, not least because it became political reality during the nineteenth century [42].

Frederick shocked Europe by his treatment of occupied Saxony, from which he raised more than one third of the entire cost borne by Prussia during the Seven Years War [286]. In response the Emperor passed an 'imperial execution' against him in 1757, which constituted a declaration of war, although the Protestant power of veto in the Imperial Diet spared Frederick the imperial ban [247]. Facing a European alliance including Austria, France and Russia, he narrowly escaped the destruction of his country and the dismemberment of his state in a peace that restored the pre-war status quo in 1763 [14, 281, 289].

His strategy of collecting clients, particularly among North Germany's smaller princes, whom he had previously denounced as opportunistic mercenaries, intensified in the second half of his reign. With renewed appreciation for Brandenburg's electoral status, the king ordered a more active policy in the imperial circles when his interests were at stake. This policy culminated with the 1785 Prussian-led League of Princes, which was directed against Habsburg plans to exchange possessions in the Netherlands with Bavaria, and which fully revealed the contradictions inherent in Frederick's policies towards the Empire [288, 290]. He could not be the protector of 'German liberties' while despising the constitution that preserved them, nor could he claim to be working for the interest of the Empire while threatening its princes.

Frederick's aggression in the Empire found a direct parallel in the king's negative policies towards Poland-Lithuania. After the incorporation of Silesia, the annexation of Polish Prussia proved the next step towards the territorial 'completion' that Frederick had planned in his 'political daydreams' [225; 369–77]. In both cases he used the law to his advantage and ignored it when it stood in the way of his aims. This parallel perspective features rarely in a historiography that divides into specialists of the Empire and those of Polish history. Some biographies of Frederick either ignore his role in the partitions of Poland entirely, or find it barely worth mentioning [235, 249]. A book published to commemorate the 200th anniversary of the king's death lists among its chapter headings 'Frederick the Great and Russia', and even 'Frederick the Great and the United States of America', but none mentions Frederick's relationship with his Polish neighbour [230]. At the other extreme, Polish and East German historians of the Communist period focused almost exclusively on Frederick's partitioning policies, thus – wholly unconvincingly – trying to discharge Russia of any responsibility [240, 264].

A more comprehensive view must take into account that the Prussian expansion into Poland, planned in detail by Ewald Friedrich von Hertzberg, one of Frederick's most influential advisers, was directly linked to Prussian–Austrian rivalry in the Empire [260].

Austria's annexation of Polish Zips (Spisz), in 1769, whetted Prussia's appetite for a similar adventure in Poland. Maria Theresa overcame her moral scruples, hoping that territorial compensation for the Hohenzollerns in Poland would leave the Empire more open to Habsburg territorial schemes.

At the same time, Russia was deeply suspicious of Prussia's hegemonic ambitions, a sentiment which motivated it to join the anti-Prussian alliance during the Seven Years War. In 1758, Russian troops occupied Königsberg, planning to unite East Prussia with Russia's Polish protectorate [277]. Impressed by the Russian governor's respect for their political privileges, the Prussian estates freely swore an oath of allegiance to Tsarina Elizabeth – an act of defiance for which Frederick never quite forgave them [133]. The accession of Peter III in 1762, however, shifted Russian foreign policy and helped save Brandenburg-Prussia from destruction. It brought home to Frederick how much Prussia's survival depended on Russian good-will. Similarly, Prussian acquisitions of Polish territories were impossible without Russian consent. After the trauma of the Seven Years War – when around 180,000 of Frederick's subjects had died [307; 321] – an armed invasion of Poland was impossible. Brandenburg was Russia's junior partner: Karl Marx called it 'Russia's jackal' [276]. Frederick had little choice but to participate in Russia's conservative programme of preserving Poland-Lithuania as its protectorate. Like his father at Nystad in 1721, Frederick concluded a new alliance in 1764 to manipulate the Polish election and to maintain the Polish constitution for Russian and Prussian benefit. As Zernack puts it, the 'miracle of the house of Brandenburg' in 1763 was directly linked to the 'debacle of the Republic of Poland' [294; 20].

New possibilities, however, soon offered themselves. As Poland-Lithuania began a cautious reform programme under its new Russian-backed monarch, Stanisław August Poniatowski (r. 1764–95), Prussia's hostile economic policies strangulated Polish trade, and Prussian troops illegally occupied the Danzig suburbs and the mouth of the Vistula. In 1770, Frederick erected a military *cordon sanitaire* across Polish Prussia under the pretext of containing the plague from spreading into Prussia. His troops requisitioned local resources to such an extent that whole villages were deserted, while men of suitable age were coerced into the Prussian army. The market was swamped with inferior Prussian currency, systematically destroying Poland's finances, which should have flourished due to rising European demand for grain. The destruction of the Polish economy was the result of years of targeted Prussian exploitation of a country politically and militarily on its knees. It was then that the picture of ruined Polish villages and towns was consciously associated with the stereotype of the disorderly 'Polish Economy', which served as a propaganda tool well into the twentieth century [235; 184–9]. The treatment of Polish Prussia reflected Frederick's opinion of the Poles: ruled by anarchy, he claimed, 'this is the last nation of Europe'. In his testament of 1768, Frederick announced he would consume Polish Prussia 'like an artichoke, [eating it] leaf by leaf' [225; 665].

The suggestion, advanced even by Frederick's recent biographers, that he did not intend or plan the partition of Poland, is bizarre, as he admitted himself that he wanted to maintain Polish 'anarchy' until '[its] powerful neighbours came to an agreement on how to divide the prey' [237; 483]. While he was dispatching his troops to occupy the territories assigned to him in the first partition treaty, he knew he had achieved the greatest success of his political career, yet he tried to play it down: 'It is a good acquisition ... but to attract less jealousy I say to anyone who might listen that during my travels there I saw nothing but sand, pine trees, heathland and Jews' [282]. Frederick's justification, later accepted by Borussian historiography, that Polish Prussia was 'returned' to Brandenburg-Prussia after more than 300 years under 'foreign, Polish rule', is absurd. The province had never been in Hohenzollern possession; the dynasty never considered itself the heir of the Teutonic Knights, but rather their enemy. The Prussian government treated Polish Prussia like a new conquest, not a long-lost province. The most convincing summary of Prussia's destructive influence can be found in Hans-Jürgen Bömelburg's detailed analysis of the Prussian occupation of the province which Frederick renamed 'West Prussia' after 1772. Many historians have uncritically followed Frederick's bureaucrats' rose-tinted picture of the Prussian take-over of the province, ignoring the well-documented protests of the population against 'Berlin despotism' [21; 235].

In its Constitution of 1791 the Polish-Lithuanian Commonwealth proved – too late – that it had the ability to pass reforms against all the odds [273]. Hiding behind the rhetoric of reason of state, the partitioning powers destroyed a member of the European family which had successfully modernised its constitution. Prussian minister Hertzberg admitted that the partitions prevented the recovery of a commonwealth that threatened to return as a serious competitor in north-east Europe [345]. In the partitions of Poland the primacy of foreign policy not only formalised Russian and Prussian domination; by wiping out the most constitutional counter-model to their own absolute monarchies, the alliance of the 'three black eagles' instituted a political conservatism which remained a major obstacle to constitutional reforms in Central Europe until the collapse of the status quo in 1917–18 [293].

6 Enlightenment and the Public Sphere

The definition of Enlightenment has become much broader since the 1970s. What had been considered a 'movement' focused around a few Parisian intellectuals splintered: as J.G.A. Pocock writes: 'Enlightenment was, and Enlightenments were as we find it and them' [342; 107]. Recently, historians have returned to more cohesive patterns, identifying various 'brands' of Enlightenment, such as the Protestant and the Catholic, the 'early' and the 'radical' Enlightenments, while various distinct 'national' Enlightenments have been identified [325, 326, 333, 343]. A 'western' rational Enlightenment, based on the French model has been distinguished from a Central European 'Counter-Enlightenment', but this dichotomomy has been convincingly queried [321, 335, 353]. The period usually called the European Enlightenment cannot be seen as one coherent ideological movement.

Prussia's Enlightenment has frequently been presented as a paradox. It is often personified in the contradictory shape of Frederick II, the aggressive militarist and conqueror, yet at the same time the philosopher, flautist and patron of the arts. Frederick is also seen as one of the definitive enlightened absolutists, a term which is itself a paradox for modern liberal democrats. Originally coined by the French physiocrats in the 1760s, *'despote éclairé'* described a ruler who, according to the Saxon cameralist Johann Heinrich von Justi (1717–71), did 'everything for the people but nothing by the people' [112; 108]. This immediately exposes the dilemma inherent in the formula 'enlightened absolutism', combining the Enlightenment precept of individual emancipation from the bondage of tradition and ignorance with the demand for subjection to a ruler whose priority was above all to consolidate the power and efficiency of his state.

This chapter engages with a contradiction which most eighteenth-century proponents of the concept apparently did not see. Did the very agency of a monarch above the law not negate the enlightened character of his reforms? In other words, was Enlightenment decreed from above true Enlightenment? As eighteenth-century Prussia also experienced the growth of a politically and socially alert public sphere, did the participants of this sphere represent a different and more genuine form of Enlightenment from below? Finally, does the revision of the paradigm of absolutism not also demand a re-thinking of the nature of the Prussian Enlightenment? [320; 1–21].

The roots of Prussian enlightened absolutism lie in the late seventeenth century. The philosopher and historian Samuel Pufendorf (1632–94) prepared the way through his radical separation of metaphysics from political thought. Under the dual influence of Hobbes's negative anthropology ('man is man's wolf') and Grotius's repositioning of the foundations of natural law from divine origins to human reason (as the source of human laws), Pufendorf saw government and the commonwealth as human creations that serve public security and protect human sociability. The basis of this commonwealth was the contract to which society had been subjected: 'the decision as to how to secure [the benefit of all] resides in those who have subjected their will to the will of the king ... to whose judgement and conscience the government has been entrusted' [332; 192]. Pufendorf's belief in the identity between the sovereign's welfare and that of the whole community is reflected in Frederick II's understanding of the state as a contract between the ruler and the ruled, and of his own role as the 'first servant of the state'. As a result, the emphasis shifted from the contribution that the ruler made to the common good, to Frederick II's belief that the happiness of a ruler depended on the welfare of his subjects: 'the sovereign represents the state, he and his people form one body which cannot be happy if they are not united by concord ... he must see, think and act for the whole community to procure all the advantages for which it is receptive' [370; 22].

A further attack on the metaphysical philosophy of politics came from Pufendorf's pupil, Christian Thomasius (1655–1728), founding rector of the University of Halle, who asserted the crucial role of human will in the formulation of law, and the inability of human reason to explore the transcendent [313]. The most important figure who exerted philosophical influence on Frederick, however, was Christian Wolff (1679–1754), a pupil of Gottfried Wilhelm Leibniz

(1646–1716), banned from Halle University by Frederick William I in 1723 and recalled by Frederick in 1740. Although Wolff elevated rigid rationalism to doctrinal status, he also revived the link between reason and the metaphysical in his *German Metaphysics*: 'a rational man accomplishes good because it is good and refrains from evil because it is evil: in which case he is similar to God, who has no superior to obligate him ... through the perfection of his nature.' [332; 267].

The Wolffian Enlightenment thus formulated progress as the striving of human beings for the perfection of their reason, in harmony with God's perfect intellect. This philosophy suited the Prussian monarch. As a Deist he believed that God, after creating the world, no longer exercised care over it, and that rationality was the best instrument to prevent the anarchy to which human beings were prone. Wolff had formulated an alternative religion of rationalism which Frederick could perfectly apply to his self-perception as philosopher king: he was the only law-giver, no longer justified by divine right but by his superior wisdom and human perfection. His ministers and politicians were merely 'instruments in the hands of a wise and competent master' [280; 157].

The formula of 'enlightened absolutism' is often seen as encapsulated in Frederick's self-description as the 'first servant of the state'. The term 'state' is especially problematic since it is often understood in an anachronistic sense, not as a contract or the 'product or construct of a specific society', but as a universal idea or a spiritual entity, in a Hegelian or Rankean sense [107; 20]. A focus on the history of institutional centralisation has reinforced this idealist notion of the Prussian 'state' under the disciplining rule of its monarch [86, 94]. Historians presented the reform activities of this eighteenth-century state as the high watermark of enlightened absolutism, but if we take a closer look, the picture is less clear: Frederick William I was a much more fundamental reformer of Prussia's institutions than his son, but he was never considered enlightened [63, 68, 336; 242].

This perspective also ignores 'non-absolutist' modernisation projects such as the Polish constitution of 3 May 1791, which was strongly influenced by Enlightenment ideas. For many historians, especially those under Marxist influence, who associate the Enlightenment with the bourgeoisie, noble-inspired reforms such as those in Poland are irrelevant [96]. The enlightened impulses which emanated from the constitution of 1791 were also supported by many West Prussian noblemen whose lands had fallen to Prussia in 1772.

The republican culture these nobles brought with them not only rejected absolutism but invigorated local political life to a degree unknown in provinces where Hohenzollern rule had reduced local political activities to a minimum. In the long term, the cooperation which developed between enlightened bureaucrats and West Prussian elites fed positively into the reforms that restored the country after the military defeats inflicted by the French armies in 1806/7 [21; 470–74, 132].

At the same time, the Realpolitik of 'enlightened absolutism' was a series of measures which often contradicted each other, and which themselves originated in political ideas and traditions pre-dating the eighteenth century. The problem of the relationship between the monarch's reformist will and the growth of an enlightened public sphere, however, is best demonstrated through these central themes of the Prussian Enlightenment: religion and toleration, and educational and legal reforms.

[i]   Pietism, Educators and the Enlightenment

General accounts of the Enlightenment traditionally stressed its anti-religious nature, yet the arrival of enlightened ideas in Prussia was closely associated with a religious movement. Pietism had emerged as response to the traumas of the Thirty Years War. Calling for the improvement of the moral fabric of society, it stressed individual over collective piety and sought a permanent reformation to be achieved through the education of the young. Pietists criticised the ossified structures of the established Lutheran church and attacked Lutherans' narrow focus on Aristotelian metaphysics. [159]. The movement reached Brandenburg-Prussia from the Empire. Its founder, Philip Jakob Spener (1635–1705), came from Württemberg, while two of its significant early supporters, August Hermann Francke (1663–1727) and the firebrand Thomasius arrived in Brandenburg after being expelled from their university posts in Leipzig, to join the new University of Halle, founded in 1694. To realise their vision of a more individualist, spiritual version of Christianity, the Pietists established conventicles in Halle, Berlin and Königsberg. Crucially they gained the support of Elector Frederick III, who saw them as useful allies against the strictly Lutheran Prussian estates.

The Pietists were no outright champions of Enlightenment, but they shared with leading enlightened thinkers a concern for the perfection of the individual and society. Francke's teaching was disseminated through the establishment of a Pietist printing press. His founding of the Halle orphanage and of schools with the provision of boarding and other support for poor students anticipated the Enlightenment interest in social welfare, but his ideas were also welcomed by a heavily indebted government, which had to rebuild territories hit by plague and famine, as in Ducal Prussia after 1709. Supported by tax breaks and other privileges, Francke's institutions in Halle began to flourish, though they were regarded with hostility by the Lutheran establishment [152, 153]. Church visitations by Pietist state and church officials implemented control and disciplined local practice [154]. From 1729, the king prevented anyone from taking up a church appointment if he had not studied at the Pietist-dominated University of Halle for at least two years. The foundation of Pietist workhouses and governmental ordinances banning all begging in the streets complemented each other.

In Ducal Prussia, Pietism proved not only a useful tool against orthodox Lutherans but also against the Catholic minority, which lost the protection of the Polish crown in 1657 (see Chapter 5). Fifty years later, Frederick William I's restructuring programme focused particularly on north-eastern areas with a Lithuanian population, where the training of teachers and preachers in the Lithuanian language advanced with Pietist support: in 1718, Lithuanian and Polish theological seminaries were founded at Königsberg University, and in 1724 the Pietitsts published a New Testament in Lithuanian [29; 127–28, 93].

Frederick William I's general support for Pietism has led several historians to revise the traditional view of him as a philistine, exclusively interested in military affairs and strict Calvinism. Günter Birtsch pointed out that the king fostered the natural sciences at the Berlin Academy, set up a College of Medicine and Surgery (1723), founded the Charité hospital in Berlin, and soon regretted his expulsion of Christian Wolff from Halle, trying to tempt him to return [316]. The king's practical approach to enlightened reforms is evident in his establishment of chairs in cameralist science at the universities of Halle and Frankfurt/Oder in 1727, intended to train future state officials in economic and legal matters. His *Rétablissement* in Eastern Prussia saw the settlement of around 10,000 exiled

Protestants from Salzburg in 1737 [173]. Despite his preference for Calvinism, he did not hesitate to settle Lutherans, Mennonites and Pietists alike, while introducing ordinances on religious peace to prevent infighting. His decree on compulsory primary schooling in 1717 was not particularly successful in practice, but was a landmark among educational developments at the time.

Unlike his father, Frederick II showed little personal interest in planting new parishes or schools, despite their extensive role in promoting the general welfare of the population. He left school reforms to his minister Johann Julius Hecker (1707–68), who founded pauper schools, established the first vocational *Realschule* and rewrote the Prussian school code in 1763. Hecker had to fear no interference from the king, who in others matters, such as war and foreign policy, never permitted such ministerial autonomy [110; 76, 339; 171–9]. In contrast, Frederick William I believed that his personal salvation depended on good governance in his role as an 'administrator for God', and his welfare-oriented brand of Pietism flourished at his spartan court in Berlin [154; 211].

Convinced that Pietism successfully promoted obedience among state officials and soldiers, Frederick William recruited Pietist chaplains for his army and applied their educational models in his new cadet academies. Though there was Pietist resistance against the rapid expansion of the army, and the darker sides of military practice – forced recruitment, maltreatment and physical punishment – challenged Pietist principles, Pietists were active in fostering military change: the leader of the Berlin Pietists, Carl Hildebrand von Canstein (1667–1719), a former army officer, proposed reforms in 1713 which included provisions for veterans, the abolition of punishment beatings, and plans to merge the standing army with the militia, foreshadowing the introduction of the Kanton Reglement of 1733 [159; 129–31] (see Chapter 3). Not all of these reforms came to fruition, but they built the foundation for changes introduced under Frederick II. Pietist influence helped produce more obedient, well-trained and usually literate soldiers, while the Pietist patronage networks, which proved attractive to army officers, developed a life of their own. They grew to control the military chaplaincy and established something of a barrier against the 'absolute state' and monarch [164].

Pietist school reforms were less successful. Compulsory schooling orders were resisted by rural parents who kept their children at home, by landlords who feared defiant subjects, and bureaucrats who would rather draft schoolmasters into the army. In Catholic areas such as Silesia the reforms were also resisted by the local clergy who believed they spread Protestant ideas. While bureaucrats wrote glowing reports on expanding teaching provision, the reality was less impressive [339; 231–8]. While the overall impact of Pietism is difficult to evaluate, Richard Gawthrop's stress on the link between Pietism and a Prussian 'spirit of subordination' needs rethinking [154; 270–84]. Most ordinary Prussians, if they noticed them at all, welcomed the benefits of Pietist social initiatives, but Lutheran Orthodoxy still dominated much of the Hohenzollern composite monarchy.

The disintegration of many Pietist networks after Francke's death in 1727 weakened the governmental symbiosis with Pietism. Yet although Frederick II's lack of interest ended official support for Pietism, its influence and institutions survived into the later eighteenth century.

[ii] Toleration?

Yet for all these affinities between Pietist and Enlightened ideas on social reform, there were indeed fundamental differences, and some of the most prominent representatives of the Prussian Enlightenment were hostile to Pietism. For Pietism and the Enlightenment had very different conceptions of human nature. For Wolff's rational human beings nothing that reason could not know could be revealed by religion. For Pietists, whose main purpose in the world was the salvation of sinful men by a mystical God who could not be known by human reason, this was close to blasphemy. Pietists accused Wolff of restricting God's omnipotence by the application of the laws of nature to the divine will [159; 292–3].

The storm was tempered with the help of a little known theologian at Halle, Siegmund Jacob Baumgarten (1706–57), who thought he could reconcile his fellow Pietists' focus on revelation with Wolff's definition of divine reason. He flagged up a common cause with the Enlightenment: the advocacy of toleration and freedom of conscience, which combined good citizenship with a tolerant practice of Christianity [349; 526]. Baumgarten's particular focus was on Christian-Jewish relations, and it is here that he exposed the narrow limits of Prussia's official toleration policies.

Jews had been banned from Brandenburg in 1573, after Joachim II's death was unjustly blamed on his Jewish master of the mint, the Jew Lippold, who was cruelly executed. Jewish settlements continued mainly in the Western territories such as Cleves. The Great Elector revoked this ban in 1669 after welcoming 50 Jewish families expelled from Austria, a policy he applied on a much larger scale to the Huguenots after 1685 [150, 151, 161]. Yet contrasts with the treatment of the Huguenots are also obvious. With settlement rights limited to 20 years, and on the whole extended only to wealthy Jews, the policy was largely motivated by fiscal considerations, since Jews were doubly burdened with excise and protection tax. After 1728 Jewish contributions were used to support Brandenburg's recruitment efforts. In contrast to the French, Jewish settlements remained tiny. By the mid-eighteenth century, only 47 Jewish families lived in the Prussian monarchy (East Prussia), 53 in Magdeburg, 168 in Pomerania, and 1,051 in Silesia [21; 425]. In 1730, Frederick William I, who had called them 'locusts' and excluded them from guild-controlled crafts, restricted their trading and property rights even further [225; 236].

Enlightened absolutism made little difference; indeed in many respects it worsened conditions for Prussian Jews. Frederick II tightened the law in 1742–4 by banning Jewish peddlers altogether, instructing local authorities to expel Jews found without protection letters. He planned to transfer whole communities from the countryside into designated walled towns [162]. After the Prussian occupation of Breslau, the number of Jewish families tolerated in the city was restricted to 12. They were given limited cultural and religious autonomy, but – in contrast to Jewish communities in Poland-Lithuania – had no political or economic autonomy. In 1744, the king abolished the Jewish rabbinical jurisdiction which had been granted to them in 1671 and 1730. When the right of no appeal came into force in 1750, they stood less chance than other Jews in the Empire, who at times quite successfully turned to the imperial court, to secure justice [32; 223, 318; 244–5]. In 1750/51 the situation further worsened for Prussia's Jews, who were divided into classes, defined by property and taxed accordingly [171]. The number of prohibitive decrees concerning Jews had tripled since 1730.

Historians of eighteenth-century Prussia usually admit that Frederician toleration excluded the Jews; yet quite recent studies still suggest that the Frederician reglement improved their situation [144].

Frederick II neither introduced legal security nor a comprehensive, unified code for Jews: the 1750 ordinance had no validity in Silesia, East Frisia, West Prussia or the territories annexed after 1793. With royal approval, several territories, such as Magdeburg or Stettin did not tolerate Jews within their walls at all.

There has been no up-to-date comparative analysis of policies towards poorer Jews across all the Hohenzollern territories, including those occupied during the first partition of Poland, where the number of Jews amounted to over 20,000, or about 10 per cent of the whole population. Large Jewish communities lived in towns and villages owned by the nobility who relied on them economically. In contrast to the small group of privileged and wealthy Court Jews of Breslau and Berlin, Polish-Prussian Jews were craftsmen, local traders and modest proprietors. On the king's orders, anyone who did not own at least 1000 thalers, was to be expelled as a 'beggarly Jew', which would have meant the expulsion of about 18,000 people [21; 422–5]. As the majority of Jewish children could not inherit protection letters, and the partitions had destroyed traditional trade networks, Jewish communities fell into poverty and were dispersed. Around 6000 Jews were expelled between 1772 and 1795 [171; 461].

The king's policies were informed by his unrealistic ideas concerning Polish Prussia's economic and social structures. A policy of randomly resettling Jewish families in small towns where they had no roots was enforced against the resistance of non-Jewish urban communities. The Jews of the Netze District were deported despite the protests of some of Frederick's own bureaucrats, not because they wanted to protect Jews, but because they knew that such measures would destroy parts of the local economy.

One of the main obstacles to a more rational policy was the king's ideological division between countryside and city, reflected in his response to the General Directory: 'There ought to be no Jews in rural areas, as Jews do not cultivate the land but engage in commerce, and commerce belongs into towns, not the countryside which must pursue agriculture, otherwise the economy does not work' [19; 436–7]. The obliteration of organically-grown structures for little obvious gain betrays not only the ignorance of a distant ruler, but also demonstrates how easily Frederick discarded enlightened theory in favour of barely-veiled prejudice.

The intervention of several local administrators against the complete removal of the Jews from the formerly Polish territories after

1772 fed Frederick's suspicions about the reliability of his bureaucratic apparatus and brought out his more autocratic tendencies. As many bureaucrats still shared anti-Jewish attitudes, however, the fate of Jews in these provinces improved only after 1812, when ideas about emancipation began to influence policy-making. While in France Jews were granted full citizenship in 1791, the Huguenot fiscal councillor for Jewish affairs in Berlin hoped that 'within three generation all Jews would have become completely assimilated to the Christians, except for a few irrelevant religious differences'. As a result he refused to implement a proposal by king Frederick William II (r. 1786–97) – not exactly famed for his support of toleration – to lighten the burden imposed on the Jews [171; 477].

If the Jews benefited from Enlightenment, they did so from their own version, the *Haskalah* (Jewish Enlightenment). Its most prominent representative was Moses Mendelssohn (1729–86), who promoted the emancipation of Jews through his philosophical treatises appealing to the Jews to abandon Yiddish. When he was elected to the Berlin Academy, however, Frederick II refused to confirm his nomination. Although Mendelssohn soon became a cultural icon for initiating a philosophical dialogue between Jews and Christians, he still had to apply for protection letters from the king to be able to keep his residence in Berlin, where he lived under permanent threat of expulsion. [348]

In 1779, the dramatist Gotthold Ephraim Lessing (1729–81) presented an enlightened parable to demonstrate the possibility of peaceful cohabitation of Christians, Jews, and Muslims by modelling the main protagonist of his drama, a Jewish merchant by the name of Nathan the Wise, on Mendelssohn, who was his personal friend. The Protestant Society of the Friends of the Enlightenment under the leadership of Friedrich Nicolai (1733–1811) co-opted Mendelssohn as an honorary member. Nicolai published the enlightened journal *Berliner Monatsschrift*, promoting Enlightened ideas at a time when reform societies and freemasonry extended into the royal house itself [328]. Lessing and Nicolai were joined in their efforts by the government official Christian Wilhelm Dohm (1751–1820), who in 1781 – the year in which Joseph II passed an emancipation decree for the Jews in the Habsburg monarchy – composed a project for the 'Civic Improvement of the Jews'. Like the Austrian reforms, the book was utilitarian in character, appealing to Jews to abandon religious doctrines and become 'useful citizens with full civic rights and duties' [323]. This approach ultimately inspired the emancipation reforms of the early nineteenth century.

Blanning's reappraisal of the German Enlightenment as 'more political than those of any other European country' is based on the observation that most enlightened writers were university professors, civil servants, diplomats, clergymen or soldiers, who actively promoted an enlightened *Kulturstaat* built on policies of religious toleration under Frederick II [315; 212–14]. Yet Blanning never comments on Frederick's attitudes towards the Jewish population, although the king's opinion about Jews is well documented in his testament of 1752, where he called them 'the most dangerous of all sects' [225; 315]. Frederick's reputation for tolerance was trumpeted by Immanuel Kant (1724–1804), Prussia's foremost philosopher at Königsberg University, in the prize-winning essay 'What Is Enlightenment?': 'A prince who does not regard it as beneath him to say that he considers it to be his duty in religious matters not to prescribe anything to his people, but to allow them complete freedom, a prince who ... is himself enlightened' [344; 58–59].

Kant qualified his statement, when he admitted that in Frederick's state the motto was: 'reason as much as you please and on what you please, but obey' [334; 11–13]. In the philosopher's mind toleration could be safely practiced only in a state that was not politically free, as freedom of conscience could undermine a body politic where obedience to the ruler's absolute power did not exist. If Kant's basic definition of Enlightenment – man's exit from self-imposed and senseless authority – is applied, then Frederick II's authority, in Kant's eyes, could not be senseless. Yet Kant could hardly have been so optimistic as to believe that his standard of tolerance would be embraced by all future Prussian rulers. If he agreed with Frederick that a ruler had no power over individual consciences, Kant could not have accepted the Prussian practice 'to have the right to tolerate Jews and, according to circumstances, expel them again', a policy that had turned repression and expulsion of Jews into legal procedure [318; 260–7]. It is only when we understand the inherent paradoxes of 'enlightened absolutism' such as this that we can grasp the character of the Prussian Enlightenment as well as its definition of toleration: both fundamentally belonged to the world of the ancien regime [106; 275–89].

Lessing, who understood that the emancipatory course of the Enlightenment would naturally collide with the sovereign's demand for obedience, disliked this Prussian paradox. In 1769 he wrote to Nicolai:

> Don't talk to me of your freedom of thought and publication in Berlin. It consists only of the freedom to publish as many idiotic attacks on religion as one wants – a freedom of which any honest man would be ashamed to avail himself. But ... let him attempt to ... stand up for the rights of the subject, to raise his voice against despotism ... and you will realise which country, up to the present, is the most slavish in Europe. [314; 175]

Lessing might have reconsidered his verdict after his move to Brunswick in 1770, when he began to publish in Berlin himself to avoid Hanoverian censorship. But he had experienced Prussian policies targeted at Silesian Catholics during his employment in Breslau in the 1760s. The 1740 annexation of Silesia added some 500,000 Catholics to the 100,000 already under Hohenzollern rule. Most lived in the Polish-speaking region of Upper Silesia, which the king's frequent travels to Silesia regularly avoided. Several Prussian policies, such as the sequestration of church properties and the conversion of monasteries into factories, corresponded to the eighteenth-century European drive to redefine the relationship between church and state. But some Prussian measures amounted to pure chicanery. Exorbitant ecclesiastical property taxes of 50 per cent, policies which disincentivised Catholics from embarking their children on ecclesiastical careers, and the abolition of asylum in ecclesiastical buildings were measures that foreshadowed the notorious nineteenth- century *Kulturkampf*. Occasionally, Frederick's pragmatism triumphed: when the Pope abolished the Society of Jesus in 1773, the king maintained the Jesuits in his own territories to avoid the closing down of schools which would have been deprived of teachers, and the desertion of the University of Breslau by Catholic students who would have chosen foreign universities over those under Prussian control. It would be misguided, however, to call this toleration.

The Silesian abbott Johann Ignaz von Felbiger (1724–88), an eminent pedagogue, was commissioned to draft the Catholic school regulation of 1765 (renewed in 1774), which introduced ideas of uniform teacher training and school books [337]. In contrast to so many of Frederick's policies in newly-conquered territories, Felbiger's reforms drew on local traditions, and – with particular relevance to Polish-speaking Upper Silesia – on the importance of bilingualism.

At times, the politics of toleration was dictated by diplomatic treaties. Prussia had guaranteed the free practice of religion for Catholics in its 1657 treaty with Poland and in the Silesian peace treaties of 1742 and 1763. Toleration – if not tolerance – thus turned into a matter of reason of state, which explains why it was extended to Christian denominations that had strong political champions but not to the Jews. By annexing Polish Prussia, the Netze District and Great Poland (New South Prussia from 1793) with their large Catholic populations, however, the Prussian monarchs were able to disregard international treaties in view of Poland's waning powers and significantly diminish the role of the Catholic church. Protestant bureaucrats imported from Pomerania and East Prussia forced priests to swear allegiance to the Prussian monarchy. Catholics became second-class citizens in every respect: they paid multiple taxation, were not admitted to administrative posts and could not purchase landed property. The Catholic church lost over two-thirds of its pre-1772 income; this blow was aggravated by an exodus of Catholic noble patrons. Travel to Poland and education in Catholic seminaries were subject to strict quotas, although state control, as usual, had its practical limits [21; 310–21, 64].

Catholics in Silesia were seen as politically unreliable, hankering after Habsburg rule; Catholics in territories of the partitions received still harsher treatment. There were no school initiatives based on Felbiger's model. In fact, school reforms introduced by the Polish Catholic Enlightenment, such as in the 1764 decree of Warmian bishop Andrzej Ignacy Baier on compulsory schooling, were repealed [29; 118]. Prussian authorities and writers projected an image that chimed with the negative views which the partitioning powers routinely disseminated about Polish 'backwardness'. Prussian distrust of the Polish Catholic nobility was intense and the cause of systematic discrimination, a fact often overlooked by analysts of the Frederician system, into which Protestant elites, mostly in the cities, assimilated more readily. Older historiography usually accepted Frederick's claim that the Polish territories were wild and disorderly, and that their Catholic inhabitants resembled uncivilised 'Iroquois' [236; 284]. While the Jewish population found several enlightened supporters of emancipation among Prussia's bureaucrats, the monarch's anti-Catholicism was generally shared by officials sent into the annexed Polish provinces. The myth of Frederick's enlightened tolerance evaporates when his actions, not his writings or his promises, are taken into account.

[iii] Law Reform

Frederick II seemed almost ubiquitous in running state affairs, travelling the country and hearing complaints from his subjects. His interest in the law was mainly directed by his suspicions about judges and the legal bureaucracy, whose personal supervision he took very seriously. He even occasionally interfered with the decisions of the highest appeal court in Berlin. As he grew older he relaxed his hands-on approach, so that the Prussian bureaucracy increasingly emancipated itself from the ruler's whims [84]. One of the most tangible reforms of his reign, in which he took interest but did not actively promote, was the General Law Code for the Prussian territories which formed Prussian legal culture throughout the nineteenth century [356]. Begun by Samuel von Cocceji, whose death in 1755 interrupted the process, it was first published in 1791 as a codification of all civil, criminal and public law. After its suspension and revision under Frederick William II in 1792, who had some of the original code's restrictions on royal prerogatives rescinded, the *Allgemeine Landrecht* 'for the Prussian states' was passed in 1794. The men who made the greatest contribution to its compilation were Johann Heinrich von Carmer (chancellor) and the lawyers Carl Gottlieb Suarez and Ernst Ferdinand Klein. Their goal was to bind absolute royal power into a purposeful and rational system of law which should 'limit individuals' freedoms only to the extent that the security and freedom of all would be protected and defended' [351].

The ambition of the Law Code's creators went beyond the ruler's desire to improve legal procedures. The king's autocratic self-image made it difficult for him to grasp the attempts by his law reformers to persuade him that arbitrary royal interference threatened the foundations of the law [355; 171–3]. The long-term objective was to harmonise the state based on law (*Rechtsstaat*) with a state dominated by bureaucracy.

The Code also sought to unify law across all Prussian territories, overruling provincial traditions, which silenced the objections Frederick William II had against its more enlightened features.

In practice, however, its claim to universality as a code for 'the Prussian state' was limited since it did not survive in the Rhenish provinces under French occupation where in 1804 the *Code Napoléon* was introduced, remaining in force after 1815 [350, 356; 49–50].

These conflicting aims produced a code full of puzzling contradictions: it applied to 'all members of [the state], without regard to their Estate, rank or gender', but also upheld the special position of the estates: 'civil society consists of many small, connected societies and estates, each of which as such ... has certain rights and duties' [351; 173]. Rights were not based on the presumption that all citizens were equal before the law – a principle only established in the 1848 constitution – but on the function and status of individuals within corporate groups [356; 55–7]. The code enshrined the exclusive noble privileges of land ownership and preferment for high office. It was a curious mixture of the traditional and the modern: most Enlightenment demands for freedom of opinion and of conscience, for the right to protection of life and property and for independent jurisdiction were guaranteed, yet the corporate privileges of ancien régime society formed the Code's underlying structure.

Reinhart Koselleck defined the period between the composition of the Law Code and the revolutions of 1848 as *Sattelzeit*, a period of transition marked by the asynchronic development of law and society – the latter changing faster than the former – which enhanced subjects' self-perception as citizens without granting them the rights that a civil society demanded. The Law Code and its makers gave perfect expression to the Prussian Enlightenment's conundrum: the rights of individuals were closely bound to the state which in the name of rationality and natural law could suspend these laws, as long as it was true to their spirit. Kant's vision of the man who was free to speak and think in public as he wished, so long as he was obedient and fulfilled his official functions, was enshrined in the letter of the Law Code.

The noble estate was consulted on the formulation of the Law Code [27; 87–125], but their representation remained subordinate and restricted to local and regional assemblies, whose role was modestly revived by governmental decree after 1788 [125, 178]. This meant that the composite character of Prussia's division in provinces and regional elites persisted. From the government's point of view, the Code reflected the triumph of the cameralist interpretation of man's 'pursuit of happiness', determined by the paternalist monarch and an increasingly powerful bureaucracy, as particular rights and immunities were prioritised over general civic laws [106; 233, 11; 201]. This authoritarian tendency is best demonstrated by the Code's implementation in the formerly Polish territories. Count Johann Carl, bishop of Warmia and a member of the Hohenzollern family, protested against Prussian officials who, armed with the Code, 'treated Polish peasants and other inhabitants of this nation with such contempt, as if they were cattle' [163; 312–17].

As societies discovered and embraced the powers of a growing public sphere, the emphasis on the subjects' usefulness to the state was supplanted by the idea of civic freedom in many states across Europe [329, 354]. Prussian enlightened absolutism and its Law Code had become an anachronism before the ink with which it was written had dried. As a practical law book for the growing bureaucracy as well as a preserver of privilege, however, it proved as lasting and adaptable as the Prussian monarchy itself.

[iv] Prussian Enlightenment and the Public Sphere

Frederick II died three years before the outbreak of the French Revolution. Prussia did not succumb to revolution. Instead a new reign started which Clark aptly called 'the most eventful and least impressive epoch' in the history of Prussia's monarchy [3; 284]. Frederick's nephew and successor, Frederick William II, was under the spell of what enlightened thinkers called spiritualist 'enthusiasm', better known as 'anti-enlightenment' [341; 280–309]. Easily influenced, he preferred religious mysticism to Wolff's rationalism and Voltaire's Deism. He did not correspond to the kingly ideal to which the law reformers had aspired. The 'language of natural law' [142] did not appeal to Frederick William, who, in most historians' eyes, was averse to reform as well as the Enlightenment. This judgement is based largely on his appointment of Johann Christoph Wöllner (1732–1800), a member of the Rosicrucian Order, as minister and confidant. Despite the king's profligacy and his adventurous love life, which produced fourteen children, he supported Wöllner's approach to religion, rewarding him with the command over the ministry of religious affairs and disproportionate influence over policy-making [244].

Bent on ending his predecessor's scepticism towards institutional religion and to restrain critical debate in the public sphere, Wöllner's

1788 Religion Edict imposed a strictly doctrinal course on all Christian denominations. It threatened clerics with legal sanctions if they taught anything in their sermons that departed from 'the body of belief of whichever religious party [they] belong to'. Wöllner's target in his words was 'bad Enlightenment', 'Deists, naturalists and other such sects' who 'abuse the name of Enlightenment'. To prevent them from 'diminishing the authority of the Bible', the king enforced the edict in tandem with a censorship decree to halt 'the perversion of fundamental Christian truths' [340; 286–91].

Despite being castigated as a reactionary, Wöllner had intellectual roots in the Enlightenment and in freemasonry. He believed that all confessions, including Catholics, Jews and Mennonites, should be tolerated so long as they did not proselytise. Writing in Nicolai's Enlightenment press he advocated a revision of Frederick's 1750 anti-Jewish edict and promoted greater rights for rural subjects, protecting them from excessive labour duties [346]. As a result, rumours spread in 1794 that the king was about to abolish serfdom; when he did not, localised uprisings broke out.

The impact of the Religion Edict was limited by a consistory that quietly boycotted some of its stricter provisions, by teachers who refused to be intimidated by it, by the university faculty at Halle which rejected the edict's authority over them, and by an emerging civil society which aired its protests publicly. It seems therefore useful to abandon the dichotomy of Enlightenment/Anti-Enlightenment altogether. Wöllner and Kant appear not a million miles apart, as both tempered their advocacy of individual freedom of expression with the demand for obedience to the state: 'The enlightened elite in Prussia ... had no problem with disciplining the masses, as long as the state reserved unto the elite a highly-restricted zone of debate, in which the latter could chew the cud of the intellectual freedom to which their educations had entitled them' [346; 9]. Against the backdrop of a large literature on the eighteenth-century public sphere, historians have sought to explain why the Prussian Enlightenment did not lead to revolution, as in France.

The answer lies in the fact that, in contrast to France, reform-minded thinkers did not work against the monarch or outside the state. The very people Blanning identified as the political activists of the Prussian Enlightenment were also its guardians against revolution. This did not make them unenlightened but it influenced the nature and definition of the Prussian Enlightenment. Wöllner was one of these guardians: he rose from a humble background through talent and service positions in the bureaucracy, promoting a slow and evolutionary Enlightenment from within and by the state, from which eventually sprang the reforms of the early nineteenth century [320; 149–65].

This version of the Enlightenment, which 'produced a lot of books but no uprising' [346; 21], contributed to Brandenburg-Prussia's stability, and it reinforced a shared identity among its elites, perhaps the most important single factor for the integration of the Hohenzollern territories at the end of the eighteenth century [331; 423–47]. It trickled down into the wider population, as elite and popular political culture drew closer to each other. Research on the 'Public Enlightenment' has focused on this newly-emerging public sphere, which embraced enlightened ideas and tolerance independently of royal reason of state and was an eminently urban, albeit not an exclusively bourgeois, event. Apart from its large garrisons, which astonished visitors, Berlin possessed salons and learned societies which raised it to the status of a European metropolis. Its growth was due not only to the civil service, but also to merchants, intellectuals, publishers, lawyers and other professionals. [317]. Berlin's Enlightenment culture was distinctly Protestant (although Jewish-run salons played a part) and not unpolitical. It supported Prussia's disputes with the Holy Roman Empire and Austria, as when Emperor Joseph II banned Nicolai's *Allgemeine Deutsche Bibliothek*. Prussia's policies against Silesian or Polish Catholics were hardly controversial. In the eyes of Kant, who praised the 'century of Frederick' as the 'age of enlightening', or Friedrich Gedike (1754–1803), a councillor of the Protestant Supreme Consistory and a pedagogical reformer, Prussia was a champion of the freedom of speech:

> It is important whether the enlightened part of the population is larger than the unenlightened; but it is even more important whether the enlightened part is allowed to write about ... the state's government and finally the rulers themselves ... as it happens here daily. ... This is all one can ask for. For so long we dreamed that the enlightened ones could speak up. And this desire, it seems to me, has been fulfilled here and nowhere else. [347; 31–2]

The public intellectual sphere had internalised the contradictions and limitations of the Prussian Enlightenment. The General Law

Enlightenment and the Public Sphere

Code and Kantian philosophy had introduced the language of civil society and the autonomy of the individual before the excesses of the French Revolution caused a political backlash [331; 447–66]. During the French revolutionary wars from 1792 to 1807, a deep-seated fear of revolution motivated Prussian policy-making, which, despite the bureaucracy's strong identification with Prussia's enlightened 'modernity', hampered its ability to promote fundamental social and constitutional reform, and stimulated its paternalist resistance to participatory constitutional models. In foreign politics, the decision for neutrality in 1795 was a demonstration of this fear. In domestic terms, reform projects were not progressive 'planning of the future' but a defensive response to channel social unrest and to prevent a break-down of the 'state machine' [355]. In East and West Prussia, the Polish example of a nation that had lost its statehood in 1795 to foreign occupation carried a stark warning against what could also happen to Prussia occupied by Napoleon's armies after 1806.

Yet the debate over reform still created opportunities for the enlightened public sphere to contribute to the discussion about crisis management after 1797, when Frederick William III acceeded to the throne. Prussia's enlightenend bureaucrats had to undergo the catastrophe of defeat in 1806/7 and occupation by Napoleon's armies before translating the language of political reform into tangible action. Ultimately, their goal was not to promote citizens' individual autonomy and political participation, as Kant might have wished, but to prevent the revolution from spreading to Prussia. The war against Napoleon revitalised local estate assemblies and boosted a more cohesive Prussian identity across its composite territories. This was Napoleon's legacy: an achievement that had eluded generations of Hohenzollern rulers in their striving for a more unitary state.

Conclusion

The rulers of Brandenburg and monarchs of Prussia were keenly aware of the composite nature of the Brandenburg-Prussian state. Political practice in this conglomerate demanded continuous negotiation, compromise and cooperation, which neither the concept of dualism between the ruler and his provincial elites, nor that of absolutism satisfactorily capture [91; 348]. How far did the integration of Hohenzollern provinces go before the French Revolution and the Napoleonic wars, when redrawn borders raised a new set of issues for Prussia's state-builders? Just as the expanding European Union today struggles to find a common economic, legal, military, cultural and political language and purpose, Prussia in the late eighteenth century found it hard to find common ground between its composite parts.

Due to the fragmentation of the Hohenzollern territories, their rulers were particularly sensitive to issues of security and the 'jealousy of our neighbours', as Frederick I put it in his testament [225; 218]. This sentiment is echoed in the writings of his successors, particularly Frederick II, who thereby justified the priority he gave to military matters, and the aggressive expansion with which he sought to establish the stability he so craved. Prussia's near destruction during the Seven Years War, caused by its own aggression, seemed to confirm Frederick's concerns.

If there was a 'minimalist' integrationist programme, one must ask whether it consciously sought to create more than an 'institutional state', held together by the army, the dynasty, administrative centralisation and a common foreign policy before one can judge the extent to which it was successful. In the age of Johann Gottfried Herder, was there a Prussian 'nation'? Was the doctrine of cameralism and the 'well-ordered police state' enough to elicit loyalty across provincial borders? Could a state of subjects and vassals – whether

Conclusion

noble, rural or urban – develop a cohesive patriotic consciousness based on liberty, active citizenship, the rule of law and a shared identity with a common *patria* (fatherland)? The provincial estates, which had fulfilled some of these functions in the sixteenth century, had by the early eighteenth century been reduced to local assemblies without policy-making powers. Traditional historiography dominated by the 'myth of absolutism' might have overestimated their loss of influence, but Neugebauer's thesis of the 'permanence of the estates' [27], while demonstrating their continued influence on local political and economic matters, fails to show that they had a powerful role in forming the rulers' central policies.

The trappings of monarchic self-representation, displayed before the people in the coronation ceremonies of 1701, did not foster integrative sentiments, particularly as the estates and their notions of participatory citizenship were consciously excluded. Other positive integrative instruments, offered and applied by the monarchy, such as Pietism, the limited toleration of religious diversity, career access for provincial elites, noble protection policies and education reforms, reduced tension but did not necessarily foster a sense of common purpose and identity with the unitary state. Changing legal and political norms and the monopoly of taxation could only be enforced with a degree of elite cooperation, but it remains an open question whether it was accompanied by any new loyalty to the state as a sum of all its provinces. There are glimpses of noble behaviour testifying to a consciousness that extended beyond their province, reflected in the heavy sacrifices during Frederick's military campaigns, which are not satisfactorily explained by a traditional emphasis on a supposed Lutheran or 'Prussian spirit' of subservience.

Eighteenth-century Prussian bureaucrats tried hard to promote the vision of a unitary Prussian nation. The example of the French national assembly, the estates general and the pursuit of 'liberty, fraternity and equality' were at first positively received in enlightened circles, although the excesses of the revolutionary activities, particularly after the 1793 execution of Louis XVI, soon struck terror into the hearts of European rulers. Frederick II's minister Hertzberg would not have accepted Herder's ideas of equality and participatory government, but he still borrowed Herderian ideas when in 1782 he described the Prussian 'national character' as martial, powerful and industrious, on a par with the great 'nations of antiquity' [232; 41]. Prussian poetry after the Seven Years War had first produced similar glorifications of 'king and fatherland' and a cult of death, which referred to the 'Prussian fatherland', rather than a provincial one. Writers associated with the enlightened public sphere were the vanguards of such literature, but they also asked whether the Prussian monarchy was a fatherland worth dying for. This active reflection on patriotism and sacrifice had the potential to turn subjects into true citizens. In the light of constitutional debates about new modes of representation during the American and French Revolutions, the limited corporate character of the estates and their lack of broad representational legitimacy were debated across the Holy Roman Empire and did not bypass Brandenburg-Prussia. Notions of the estates as socially and economically defined groups, which might extend into larger urban and rural populations, slowly started to undermine older notions of their role as political corporations [36, 132]. New criteria for a citizenship of all free and propertied men appeared on the horizon [141; 301–3].

Yet for all this debate, Prussia's political and constitutional development did not make this transition to modern citizenship. Kant's hope in the slow germination of the 'seed of freedom', cultivated by enlightened writers, was barely noted by the leading Prussian bureaucrats or the makers of the 1794 Law Code. It is no accident that Kant championed representative politics from his chair in Königsberg, not far from West Prussia, where the memory of extensive liberties of the estates survived the partitions of Poland, and even nearer to Courland, Livonia and Estonia, where in 1796 Tsar Paul I reinstated the political domination of the estates. Kant had observed the transition to a new notion of citizenship in what was left of Poland in 1791, where the Diet finally concluded wide-ranging reforms while Russia and Prussia were distracted by warfare in the East and West. If in Prussia demands for the convocation of provincial estate assemblies were routinely declined until the later 1790s, the terms of the debate in local and regional assemblies provide glimpses of an underlying shift towards more fundamental social and political reforms in the Hohenzollern provinces initiated by the estates, which transcended a purely local outlook and, as in West Prussia, included demands for the abolition of serfdom. Prussia's decision to conclude the peace of Basel with Napoleon in 1795 to have a free hand in Poland's third partition and elimination from

Conclusion

the map of Europe, however, meant that domestic political reform and liberalisation in Prussia were further delayed. The implementation of constitutional monarchy in Poland looked so threatening to the partitioning powers that the suppression of a Polish rump state that looked governable again took priority over everything else. This meant, however, that unitary citizenship based on property, which not only had the potential to integrate provinces but also to break down barriers between the noble and urban populations, had to wait until after 1806/7, when Prussia's crushing defeat by Napoleon demonstrated the need for fundamental reform. Prussia remained a composite state because it only succeeded in winning over part of its elites, in some of its territories to the drive towards a unitary state. It failed to create a unitary national identity before the nineteenth century because – although it gave its subjects a state based on law – it failed to concede a participatory constitution creating the basis for modern citizenship on the model of the European Enlightenment.

Appendix 1: A Selective Genealogy of the Brandenburg and Prussian Hohenzollern Lines, 1415–1797

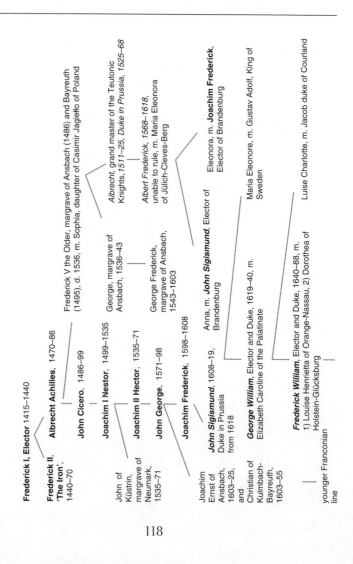

Frederick III, Elector and Duke, 1688–1701/1713, as *Frederick I*, king in Prussia 1701–13, m. 1) Elizabeth Henrietta of Hesse-Kassel, 2) Sophia Charlotte of Hanover, sister of George I of Britain, 3) Sophia Louise of Mecklenburg-Schwerin

Frederick William I, king in Prussia, 1713–40, son of 2), m. Sophia Dorothea of Hanover, daughter of George I of Britain

Frederick II, king of Prussia 1740–86, m. Elizabeth Christine of Brunswick-Bevern

Louise Ulrike, m. Adolf Frederick, King of Sweden

Henry, prince of Prussia, d. 1802

August William, prince of Prussia, d. 1758, m. Louise Amalie of Brunswick-Lüneburg

Frederick William II, king of Prussia, 1786–97, m. 1) Elizabeth Christine of Brunswick-Lüneburg, 2) Frederika Louise of Hesse-Darmstadt

Frederick William III, king of Prussia, 1797–1840, son of 2), m. Louise of Mecklenburg-Strelitz

Electors are marked in bold, dukes/kings in Prussia in italics. M. = married, d.= died

Appendix 2: Table of Offices

Central Institutions	Province	Year	Provincial Institution	Function
	Electoral Brandenburg	1516	*Kammergericht*	Highest territorial court
		1604	Privy Council	Central policy-making and jurisdiction
		1630–41	War Council	Collected war contributions
		1652	*Amtskammer*	Centrally appointed officials
	Cleves-Mark	1653	*Amtskammer*	
	Eastern Pomerania	1654	*Amtskammer*	
		1661	*Hofgericht*	Highest territorial court
	Ducal Prussia	1656	War Chancery	
		1661	*Amtskammer*	
		1661	*Obertribunal*	Highest territorial court
	Magdeburg	1680	*Amtskammer*	
Generalkriegskommissariat (General War Commissariat)		1660		Coordinated all territorial war chanceries and commissariats

Akzise (Excise)	Brandenburg 1667	
	Halberstadt 1672	
	Prussia 1674	
	Minden 1674	
	Pomerania 1682	
	Magdeburg 1685	
	Cleves/Mark 1716/20	
Hofkammer	1689	Except Brandenburg and Ducal Prussia	Highest appeal court
Oberappellationsgericht (new form of *Hofkammer*)	1703	Except Ravensberg, Ducal Prussia and the Mark Brandenburg, which had their own highest law courts (*Kammergericht/Obertribunal*)	Highest appeal court after privilege of no appeal (to the Emperor) 1703: but did not cover all territories
Generalfinanz-Direktorium (General Finance Directory)	1713		Ruled over provincial *Amtskammern*
Generaldirektorium (General Directory)	1723	Domain officials remain under control of local estates	Supervised Domaine Chambers (*Amts- und Domänenkammern*) at provincial level
Department of Foreign Affairs	1728		
Cabinet in Potsdam	After 1720s		The king ruled from within a cabinet of personally chosen advisers

Select Bibliography

General Works and Interpretations on Brandenburg-Prussia

[1] J. Breuilly (ed.), *Nineteenth-century Germany: Politics, Culture and Society 1780–1918* (London, 2001), is a clearly-structured introduction to the topic.
[2] F.L. Carsten, *The Origins of Prussia*, 3rd ed. (Oxford, 1964), marked a major turn against the state-focused history of the Borussian tradition.
[3] C. Clark, *Iron Kingdom: The Rise and Downfall of Prussia, 1600–1947* (London, 2006). Brilliantly written, up-to-date prizewinning account. Its size should not deter.
[4] J.G. Droysen, *Geschichte der preußischen Politik* (14 vols, Leipzig, 1855–86), is representative of Borussian historiography.
[5] P. Dwyer (ed.), *The Rise of Prussia 1700–1830* (Harlow, 2000). Good articles by Berger, Scott, Melton and van Zande.
[6] S. Haffner, *Preußen ohne Legende*, 2nd ed. (Hamburg, 1979), is an essayistic, thought-provoking work, which changed perceptions of Prussia in post-war Germany.
[7] G. Labuda et al. (eds), *Historia Pomorza*, 4 vols, vol II: parts 1–3, 1454/66–1648/57, 1657–1815 (Poznań, 1976, 1984, 2003), presents the Polish understanding of Pomerania as 'land on the Baltic sea', from west Pomerania to the border with Lithuania.
[8] W. Neugebauer, *Die Hohenzollern*, 2 vols (Stuttgart, 1996, 2003), is a traditional history of the Hohenzollern dynasty.
[9] W. Neugebauer, *Geschichte Preußens* (Hildesheim, Zürich, New York, 2004), provides an interpretative survey with a good selection of literature in German.
[10] V. Press, *Kriege und Krisen. Deutschland 1600–1715* (Munich, 1991). A textbook on military and political history.
[11] H. Rosenberg, *Bureaucracy, Aristocracy and Autocracy: The Prussian Experience 1660–1815* (Harvard, 1966). Good example of the *Sonderweg* school, which attributes great importance to the alliance between Prussian rulers and their noble elites.
[12] S. Salmonowicz, *Preussen. Geschichte von Staat und Gesellschaft* [1985], German trans. (Herne, 1995), provides a differentiated image of Prussia, opposed to older national interpretations.

Select Bibliography

[13] H.M. Scott, B. Simms (eds), *Culture of Power in Europe during the Long Eighteenth Century* (Cambridge, 2007), esp. articles by Scott, Clark and Wilson.
[14] H. M. Scott, *The Emergence of the Eastern Powers, 1756–1775* (Cambridge, 2001). Detailed analysis of foreign policy relations in central and north-east Europe, with a particular focus on Prussia.
[15] J. Sheehan, *German History 1770–1866* (Oxford, 1989), usually frightens students with its detail and dense style, but is eminently useful.
[16] B. Wachowiak, A. Kamieński, *Dzieje Brandenburgii-Prus na progu czasów nowożytnych (1500–1701)* (Poznań, 2001), focuses on the early centuries of the history of Brandenburg-Prussia, with a comprehensive overview of Polish historiography.
[17] M. Wienfort, *Geschichte Preussens* (Munich, 2008). A rather superficial survey on state-building and foreign policy.
[18] P. H. Wilson, *From Reich to Revolution. German History, 1558–1806* (Basingstoke, 2004). The most useful textbook on the history of the Holy Roman Empire during that period.

Specific Regions and Provinces

[19] M. Bär, *Westpreußen unter Friedrich dem Großen*, 2 vols (Leipzig, 1909), here 2/2. Classic archive-based work on the annexation of Polish Prussia by Frederick II, trying hard not to demolish the king's shining reputation.
[20] F. Beck, K. Neitmann (eds), *Brandenburgische Landesgeschichte und Archivwissenschaft. Festschrift für Lieselott Enders* (Weimar, 1997). Essays on the regional history of Brandenburg, esp. by Peters and Neugebauer.
[21] H.-J. Bömelburg, *Zwischen polnischer Ständegesellschaft und preussischem Obrigkeitsstaat. Vom Königlichen Preussen zu Westpreussen (1756–1806)* (Munich, 1995) challenges the positive verdict on Frederick II's annexation of Polish Prussia (against Bär), raising awareness of a much neglected topic.
[22] L. Enders, *Die Altmark. Geschichte einer kurmärkischen Landschaft in der Frühneuzeit* (Berlin, 2008).
[23] K. Friedrich, *The Other Prussia. Prussia, Poland and Liberty, 1569–1772* (Cambridge, 2000), focuses on the identity and political role of the urban and noble estates of Polish Prussia.
[24] D. Kirby, *Northern Europe in the Early Modern Period: The Baltic World, 1492–1772* (Harlow, 1990), provides valuable context.
[25] I. Materna, W. Ribbe (eds), *Brandenburgische Geschichte* (Berlin, 1995), summarises the history of Brandenburg for a scholarly and a wider audience.
[26] C. Mylius (ed.), *Corpus Constitutionum Marchicarum*, 11 vols (Berlin, Halle, 1737), vol. 1, no. 12.
[27] W. Neugebauer, *Politischer Wandel im Osten. Ost- und Westpreußen von den alten Ständen zum Konstitutionalismus* (Stuttgart, 1992), challenges the

Select Bibliography

thesis that eighteenth- and nineteenth-century estates in Brandenburg-Prussia had no influence on policy-making.

[28] C. Nolte, *Familie, Hof und Herrschaft. Das verwandtschaftliche Beziehungs- und Kommunikationsnetz der Reichsfürsten am Beispiel der Markgrafen von Brandenburg-Ansbach (1440–1530)* (Ostfildern, 2005), presents Franconian kinship policies.

[29] E. Opgenoorth (ed.), *Handbuch der Geschichte Ost- und Westpreußens*, 4 vols (Lüneburg, 1994–8), here II/2 (Lüneburg, 1996), is a failed attempt to present Polish and German historiography on equal terms.

[30] E. Opgenoorth, 'Die rheinischen Gebiete Brandenburg-Preußens im 17. und 18. Jahrhundert', P. Baumgart (ed.), *Expansion und Integration. Zur Eingliederung neugewonnener Gebiete in den preußischen Staat* (Vienna, 1984). A useful collection of essays on Brandenburg-Prussian expansion and integration policies.

[31] M. Toeppen (trans. M. Szymańksa-Jasińska, ed. Grzegorz Jasiński), *Historia Mazur* [1870] (Olsztyn, 1998). A regional history of the Mazurian region by a historian who knew nineteenth-century local archives.

[32] Gabriela Wąs, 'Śląsk pod panowaniem Pruskim', M. Czapliński (ed.), *Historia Śląska* (Wrocław, 2002), 118–248, focuses on Prussian Silesia as part of an up-to-date multi-authored history of the province.

History of Historiography

[33] U. Arnold, 'Geschichtsschreibung im Preußenland bis zum Ausgang des 16. Jahrhunderts', *Jahrbuch für Geschichte Mittel- und Ostdeutschlands* 19 (1971), 74–126, focuses on late medieval historiography.

[34] S. Berger, 'Prussia in history and historiography from the eighteenth to the nineteenth century', in [5], 27–44, gives a succinct summary of the main currents of history-writing about Prussia.

[35] G. Birtsch, 'Pflichthandeln und Staatsräson. Der Gründer des preußischen Staats Kurfürst Friedrich Wilhelm im Spiegel der Geschichtsschreibung', in [70], 137–49, provides a complimentary view of Frederick William with a useful summary of older historiography.

[36] H.-J. Bömelburg, 'Die königlich preußische bzw. westpreußische Landesgeschichte in der Frühen Neuzeit – Probleme und Tendenzen. Eine Streitschrift', *Nordost-Archiv. Zeitschrift für Regionalgeschichte* NF VI/2 (1997), 607–28. A polemical exchange with [132] on the evaluation of representative traditions.

[37] K. Friedrich, '"Pomorze" or "Preussen"? Polish perspectives on early modern Prussian history', *German History* 22/3, Special Issue (K. Friedrich, ed.): Views of German History (2004), 344–71. Introduces Polish historiography across a wide chronological range.

[38] P.-M. Hahn, *Friedrich der Große und die deutsche Nation. Geschichte als politisches Argument* (Stuttgart, 2007), critically assesses the 'legend of Frederick II'.

Select Bibliography

[39] W. Neugebauer, 'Otto Hintze und seine Konzeption der allgemeinen Verfassungsgeschichte der neueren Staaten', *Zeitschrift für Historische Forschung* 20 (1993), 65–96, discusses Hintze's importance for European constitutional history.

[40] J. Sarnowsky, 'Land und Städte: Ansätze zu einer Sozial- und Wirtschaftsgeschichte Preußens im 14. und 15. Jahrhundert', *Beiträge zur Geschichte Westpreußens* 15 (1997), 27–47, on the social and economic history of the Teutonic Order.

[41] M. Toeppen, *Geschichte der preußischen Historiographie von Dusburg auf Schütz* (Berlin, 1853).

[42] B. Wehinger, 'Denkwürdigkeiten des Hauses Brandenburg. Friedrich der Große als Autor der Geschichte seiner Dynastie', G. Lottes (ed.), *Vom Kurfürstentum zum Königreich der Landstriche. Brandenburg-Preußen im Zeitalter von Absolutismus und Aufklärung* (Berlin, 2004), 137–74.

[43] K. Zernack, 'Der historische Begriff "Ostdeutschland" und die deutsche Landesgeschichte', *Nordost-Archiv. Zeitschrift für Regionalgeschichte* NF 1 (1992), 157–73, critically surveys German approaches to the history of East Central Europe.

The Teutonic Legacy

[44] M. Biskup, G. Labuda, *Dzieje Zakonu Krzyżackiego w Prusach* (Gdańsk, 1986). An archive-based study of the Teutonic Knights in Prussia, which tries to change some of the negative perceptions of older Polish approaches.

[45] M. Biskup, 'Etniczno-demograficzne przemiany Prus Krzyżackich w rozwoju osadnictwa w średniowieczu (o tzw. nowym plemeniu Prusaków)', *Kwartalnik Historyczny* (1991), z.2, 45–67, analyses the composition of early settlements in a non-ideological way.

[46] M. Biskup, 'Do Genezy inkorporacji Prus', *Przegląd Zachodni* 10 (1954), 293–306.

[47] M. Biskup, R. Czaja (eds), *Państwo zakonu krzyżackiego w Prusach. Władza i społeczeństwo* (Warsaw 2008), an up-to-date multi-authored social, political and religious history of the Order.

[48] M. Bogucka, K. Zernack, *Sekularyzacja Zakonu Krzyżackiego w Prusach. Hołd Pruski 1525 roku* (Warsaw, 1998). A textbook with edited sources on Albrecht's 1525 homage (in German and Polish).

[49] M. Burleigh, *The German Order and Prussian Society: A Noble Corporation in Crisis, 1410–1466* (Cambridge, 1982).

[50] M. Burleigh, 'The Knights, Nationalists and the Historians: Images of Medieval Prussia from the Enlightenment to 1945', *European History Quarterly* 17 (1987), 35–55.

[51] R. Czaja, *Miasta Pruskie a Zakon Krzyżacki. Studia nad stosunkami między miastem a władzą terytorialną w późnym średniowieczu* (Toruń, 1999), revises an older negative understanding of the Teutonic Order's urban policies.

Select Bibliography

[52] Th. Hirsch (ed.), 'Die Danziger Chronik vom Bunde', Th. Hirsch (ed.), *Scriptores rerum Prussicarum* vol 4 (Leipzig, 1870), 409–48. Fifteenth-century chronicles.

[53] H. Łowmiański (M. Kosman, ed.), *Prusy – Litwa – Krzyżacy*, (Warsaw, 1989). Work by one of Poland's most eminent medieval historians on Polish–Teutonic relations.

[54] M. Perlbach, *Prussia Scholastica: die Ost-und West-Preussen auf den mittelalterlichen Universitäten* (Leipzig, 1895).

[55] J. Sarnowsky, 'Zölle und Steuern im Ordensland Preußen (1403–1454)', Z.H. Nowak (ed.), *Zakon Krzyżacki a społeczeństwo państwa w Prusach* (Toruń, 1995), 67–82.

[56] H. von Treitschke (trans. E. and C. Paul), *Origins of Prussianism* [1862] (New York, 1969), appeals to Bismarck to expand into Eastern Europe in imitation of the Teutonic Knights.

[57] W. Wippermann, *Der Ordensstaat als Ideologie* (Berlin, 1979), deconstructs the myths surrounding the Teutonic Order throughout history.

[58] Z. Zdrójkowski (ed.), *Studia Culmensia Historico-Iuridica. Księga Pamiątkowa 750–lecia Prawa Chełmińskiego*, 2 vols (Toruń, 1988–90), studies the practice of Kulm Law, esp. articles by Czacharowski and Małłek on the role of law in Teutonic, Ducal and Royal Prussia.

Composite Monarchy and 'State-building'

[59] P. Baumgart, J. Schmädeke (eds), *Ständetum und Staatsbildung in Preußen. Ein Tagungsbericht* (Berlin, 1983). An influential collection of studies on the estates in Brandenburg-Prussia's composite territories during the seventeenth and early eighteenth centuries, esp. articles by Birtsch, Hahn, Heinrich, Neugebauer and Press.

[60] B. von Bonin, 'Der Kurbrandenburgische Kriegsrat (1630–1641)', *Forschungen zur Brandenburgischen und Preussischen Geschichte* 25 (1912), 51–89.

[61] K. Breysig, 'Die Organisation der brandenburgischen Kommissariate in der Zeit von 1660–1697', *Forschungen zur Brandenburgischen und Preussischen Geschichte* 5 (1892), 135–56.

[62] H. H. Diehlmann (ed.), *Erbhuldigungen des Herzogtums Preußen*, 2 parts. Part II: 1648–78, Geheimes Staatsarchiv Preußischer Kulturbesitz, Etatministerium Titel 87d, nos. 20–38 (Hamburg, 1983).

[63] R. Dorwart, *The Administrative Reforms of Frederick William I of Prussia* (Cambridge, MA, 1953), gives a detailed summary of all reforms.

[64] M. Drozdowski, 'Der Zusammenstoß des preußischen Verwaltungssystems mit den polnischen Verwaltungstraditionen (1772–1806)', P. Nitsche (ed.), *Preußen in der Provinz. Beiträge zum 1. deutsch-polnischen Historikerkolloquium* (Frankfurt, 1991), 22–34.

[65] J. Elliott, 'A Europe of Composite Monarchies', *Past and Present* 137 (1992), 48–71. A highly influential article, focusing on Spain and Britain.

[66] B. Emich, 'Frühneuzeitiche Staatsbildung und politische Kultur. Für die Veralltäglichung eines Konzepts', B. Stollberg-Rilinger (ed.), *Was*

Select Bibliography

heißt Kulturgeschichte des Politischen? *Zeitschrift für Historische Forschung*, Beiheft 35 (2005), 191–205. Propagates a new approach to the cultural history of politics.

[67] H. Freiwald, *Markgraf Albrecht von Ansbach-Kulmbach und seine landständische Politik als Deutschordens-Hochmeister und Herzog in Preußen während der Entscheidungsjahre 1521–1528* (Kulmbach, 1961). Detailed political biography of Albrecht during his early years as duke in Prussia, but neglects relations with Poland.

[68] R. Gothelf, 'Frederick William I and the beginnings of Prussian absolutism, 1713–1740', in [5], 47–67, provides a good overview but few new insights.

[69] A. Gotthard, 'Der Große Kurfürst und das Kurkolleg', *Forschungen zur Brandenburgischen und Preußischen Geschichte* 6 (1996), 1–54.

[70] G. Heinrich (ed.), *Ein sonderbares Licht in Teutschland. Beiträge zur Geschichte des Großen Kurfürsten von Brandenburg (1640–1688), Zeitschrift für Historische Forschung*, Beiheft 8 (Berlin, 1990). A useful collection on the role of Elector Frederick William and his policies, esp. articles by Birtsch and Kunisch.

[71] O. Hintze, *Staat und Verfassung. Gesammelte Abhandlungen zur allgemeinen Verwaltungsgeschichte*, ed. Gerhard Oestreich, 3rd ed. (Göttingen, 1970). A modern edition of a classic on Prussian constitutional history.

[72] S. Isaacsohn (ed.), *Urkunden und Actenstücke zur Geschichte des Kurfürsten Friedrich Wilhelms von Brandenburg*, vol. 10 (Berlin, 1880). An extensive yet selective collection of documents on the Great Elector's reign.

[73] S. Isaacsohn, 'Die Finanzen Joachims II. und das Ständische Kreditwerk', *Zeitschrift für Preußische Geschichte und Landeskunde* 16 (1879), 455–79.

[74] H.C. Johnson, *Frederick the Great and His Officials* (New Haven, 1975), like Rosenberg, stresses the domination of a Junker bureaucracy during Prussia's rise.

[75] M. Kaiser, M. Rohrschneider (eds), *Membra unius capitis. Studien zu Herrschaftsauffassungen und Regierungspraxis in Kurbrandenburg (1640–1688)*. Forschungen zur Brandenburgischen und Preussischen Geschichte NF Beiheft 7 (Berlin, 2005), focuses on the composite character of the Hohenzollern territories, esp. articles by Burkardt, Göse, Körber, Löffler, Luh.

[76] I. Kąkolewski, 'Urzędy centralne w Brandenburgii i Prusach Książęcych w XVI i XVII wieku', A. Gąsiorowski, R. Skowron (eds), *Urzędy dworu monarszego dawnej Rzeczypospolitej i państw ościennych. Materiały z sesji zorganizowanej przez zamek królewski na Wawelu, listopad 1993* (Kraków, 1996), 73–83, discusses the role of central offices in Brandenburg-Prussia.

[77] M. Klinkenborg (ed.), *Acta Brandenburgica. Brandenburgische Regierungsakten seit der Begründung des Geheimen Rates*, vol. 1 (Berlin, 1927), 91–6.

[78] H.G. Koenigsberger, 'Dominium Regale or Dominium Politicum et Regale', H.G. Koenigsberger, *Politicians and Virtuosi: Essays in Early Modern History* (London, 1986).

Select Bibliography

[79] H.G. Koenigsberger, 'Monarchies and Parliaments in Early Modern Europe Dominium Regale or Dominium Politicum et Regale', *Theory and Society* 5/2 (1978), 191–217.

[80] V. Loewe, 'Die Allodifikation der Lehen unter Friedrich Wilhem I', *Forschungen zur Brandenburgischen und Preussischen Geschichten* 11 (1898), 41–74.

[81] O. Meinardus, *Protokolle und Relationen des Brandenburgischen Geheimen Rates aus der Zeit des Kurfürsten Friedrich Wilhelm*, 6 vols (Leipzig, 1889–1919).

[82] W. Neugebauer, 'Staatliche Einheit und politischer Regionalismus. Das Problem der Integration in der brandenburg-preußischen Geschichte bis zum Jahre 1740', W. Brauneder (ed.), *Staatliche Vereinigung: Fördernde und hemmende Elemente in der deutschen Geschichte.* Der Staat 12 (Berlin, 1998), 49–87.

[83] W. Neugebauer, 'Das preußische Kabinett in Potsdam. Eine verfassungsgeschichtliche Studie zur fürstlichen Zentralsphäre in der Zeit des Absolutismus', *Jahrbuch für brandenburgische Landesgeschichte* 44 (1993), 69–115.

[84] W. Neugebauer, 'Zur neueren Deutung der preussischen Verwaltung im 17. und 18. Jahrhundert. Eine Studie in vergleichender Sicht', *Jahrbuch für Geschichte Mittel- und Ostdeutschlands* 26 (1977), 86–127, is a prime example of institutional history.

[85] G. Oestreich, *Der brandenburg-preußische Geheime Rat vom Regierungsantritt des großen Kurfürsten bis zu der Neuordnung im Jahre 1651* (Würzburg, 1937).

[86] G. Oestreich (B. Oestreich ed.), *Strukturprobleme der frühen Neuzeit : ausgewählte Aufsätze* (Berlin, 1980). A collection of influential articles on European constitutional history. In English, see his *Neo-Stoicism and the Early Modern State* (D. McLintrock trans.) (1982).

[87] E. Opgenoorth, *"Ausländer" in Brandenburg-Preussen als leitende Beamte und Offiziere 1604–187.* Beihefte zum Jahrbuch der Albertus-Universität Königsberg/Pr. 28 (Würzburg, 1967).

[88] J. Petersohn, 'Staatskunst und Politik des Markgrafen Georg Friedrich von Brandenburg-Ansbach und –Bayreuth, 1539–1603', *Zeitschrift für Bayerische Landesgeschichte* 24 (1961), 229–76.

[89] M. Raeff, *The Well-Ordered Police State: Social and Institutional Change through Law in the Germanies and Russia, 1600–1800* (New Haven, 1983). Influential work on the changing role of state ordinances.

[90] W. Reinhard (ed.), *Power Elites and State Building.* European Science Foundation Series (Oxford, 1996), provides a useful introduction on state-building approaches.

[91] M. Rohrschneider, 'Zusammengesetzte Staatlichkeit in der Frühen Neuzeit. Aspekte und Perspektiven der neuen Forschung am Beispiel Brandenburg-Preußens', *Archiv für Kulturgeschichte* 90/2 (2008), 321–49, calls for further research into the features of Brandenburg-Prussia's composite nature.

[92] F. Scheville, *The Great Elector* (Chicago, 1947) promotes the myth of Frederick William as founding father of the 'Prussian state'.

[93] F. Terveen, *Gesamtstaat und Rétablissement. Der Wiederaufbau des nördlichen Ostpreussens unter Friedrich Wilhelm I., 1714–1740* (Göttingen, 1954).

Select Bibliography

[94] A. Wakefield, *The Disordered Police State: German Cameralism as Science and Practice* (Chicago, 2009), sees the cameralists motivated mainly by self-interest.

[95] W.E.J. Weber, 'Dienst und Partizipation: Bemerkungen zur Rolle der hohen Beamtenschaft in der frühneuzeitlichen Staatsbildung', A. Mączak, W. Weber (eds), *Der frühmoderne Staat in Ostzentral-Europa* (Augsburg, 1999), 103–15. A good example of West–East comparative history-writing.

The Controversy over 'Absolutism'

[96] P. Anderson, 'Prussia', in P. Anderson, *Lineages of the Absolutist State* (London, 1974), 236–78. European 'absolutism' from a Marxist perspective.

[97] R. Asch, Heinz Duchhardt (eds), *Der Absolutismus- ein Mythos? Strukturwandel monarchischer Herrschaft in West- und Mitteleuropa (c.1550–1700)* (Cologne, 1996).

[98] P. Baumgart, 'Absolutismus ein Mythos? Aufgeklärter Absolutismus ein Widerspruch? Reflexionen zu einem kontroversen Thema gegenwärtiger Frühneuzeitforschung', *Zeitschrift für Historische Forschung* 27 (2000), 573–89.

[99] J.-B. Bossuet (ed. and trans. Patrick Riley), *Politics drawn from the Very Words of the Holy Scripture* (Cambridge, 1990). Louis XIV's main political philosopher.

[100] H. Dreitzel, *Absolutismus und Ständische Verfassung in Deutschland. Ein Beitrag zur Kontinuität und Diskontinuität der politischen Theorie in der Frühen Neuzeit* (Mainz, 1992).

[101] H. Duchhardt, 'Absolutismus – Abschied von einem Epochenbegriff', *Historische Zeitschrift* 258 (1994), 113–22, started the German debate on the 'myth of absolutism'.

[102] H. Duchhardt, 'Die Absolutismusdebatte – eine Antipolemik', *Historische Zeitschrift* 275 (2002), 323–31.

[103] N. Henshall, *The Myth Of Absolutism: Change And Continuity in Early Modern European Monarchy* (London, 1992), provocatively summarises the rethinking on 'absolutism'.

[104] J. Kunisch, *Absolutismus. Europäische Geschichte vom Westfälischen Frieden bis zur Krise des Ancien Régime* (Göttingen, 1986). Useful summary of various positions on the concept of absolutism, predating the revisionist debate.

[105] A. Landwehr, '"Normendurchsetzung" in der Frühen Neuzeit? Kritik eines Begriffs', *Zeitschrift für Geschichtswissenschaft* 48/2 (2002), 146–62. On the limits of the execution of laws.

[106] H. Reinalter, H. Klueting (eds), *Der aufgeklärte Absolutismus im europäischen Vergleich* (Vienna, 2002), esp. articles by Fuhrmann/Klippel and Gestrich on the concept of enlightened absolutism.

Select Bibliography

[107] L. Schilling (ed.), *L'absolutisme – un concept irremplaçable? Absolutismus, ein unersetzliches Forschungskonzept?* (Munich, 2008), esp. articles by Landwehr and Schilling.
[108] J. Schlumbohm, 'Gesetze, die nicht durchgesetzt werden – ein Strukturmerkmal des frühneuzeitlichen Staates?', *Geschichte und Gesellschaft* 23 (1997), H. 4, 647–63, like Landwehr [105], demonstrates the limits of early modern government.
[109] H.M. Scott (ed.), *Enlightened Absolutism. Reform and Reformers in Later Eighteenth-Century Europe* (Basingstoke, 1990). Valuable textbook on plural 'enlightened absolutisms' in Europe.
[110] R. Vierhaus (trans. J. Knudsen), *Germany in the Age of Absolutism* (Cambridge, 1988). Textbook on the subject, pre-dating revisionism.
[111] R. Vierhaus, 'Fürstlicher Absolutismus und landständischer Widerstand', in R. Vierhaus (ed. D. Groh), *Propyläen Geschichte Deutschlands, V: Staaten und Stände. Vom Westfälischen bis zum Hubertusburger Frieden 1648 bis 1763* (Berlin, 1984), 105–17.
[112] P. H. Wilson, *Absolutism in Central Europe* (London, 2000) provides clear definitions and a summary of approaches.
[113] T. Winkelbauer (eds), *Die Habsburgermonarchie 1620–1740. Leistungen und Grenzen des Absolutismusparadigmas* (Stuttgart, 2006), 301–15. One of the most important books on the composite nature of the Habsburg lands.

Estates Society

[114] S. Augusiewicz, 'Der Landtag im Herzoglichen Preußen und der Reichstag der Adelsrepublik im 16. und 17. Jahrhundert – Aspekte und Perspektiven eines Vergleichs', A. Perłakowski et al. (eds), *Die Reiche Mitteleuropas in der Frühen Neuzeit. Integration und Herrschaft. Liber memorialis Jan Pirożyński* (Cracow, 2009), 179–88. Brief comparative study of the estate assemblies in Ducal Prussia and Poland-Lithuania.
[115] P.-E. Back, *Herzog und Landschaft. Politische Ideen und Verfassungsprogramme in Schwedisch-Pommern um die Mitte des 17. Jahrhunderts* (Lund, 1955). A history of the Swedish Pomeranian estates and their political programme.
[116] J. Bahlcke et al. (eds), *Ständefreiheit und Staatsgestaltung in Ostmitteleuropa. Übernationale Gemeinsamkeiten in der politischen Kultur vom 16. –18. Jahrhundert* (Leipzig, 1999), stresses the modernising influence of estate representation in east-central Europe.
[117] F. J. Burghardt, 'Brandenburg und die niederrheinischen Stände, 1615–1620', *Forschungen zur Brandenburgischen und Preußischen Geschichte* NF 17/1 (2007), 1–95.
[118] Croy Correspondence (MS): Akten Schwerin (381.I), Nr. 186 (7), Korrepondenz mit Ernest de Croy, 1670–71, 'Brief Schwerins an Croy, 3.11.1670, p. 208, sources from the State Archives in Olsztyn, Poland.

Select Bibliography

[119] R. v. Friedeburg (ed.), *'Patria' und 'Patrioten' vor dem Patriotismus. Pflichten, Rechte, Glauben und die Rekonfigurierung europäischer Gemeinwesen im 17. Jahrhundert* (Wiesbaden, 2005). A collection of articles examining the relationship of confessionalisation, privileges and early modern patriotism.

[120] K. Friedrich, B. Pendzich (eds), *Citizenship and Identity in a multinational Commonwealth. Poland-Lithuania in Context, ca. 1550–1750* (Leiden, 2008), esp. introduction.

[121] C. Fürbringer, *Necessitas und Libertas. Staatsbildung und Landstände im 17. Jahrhundert in Brandenburg* (Frankfurt/M., 1985). A study on state–estates dualism and the policies of reason of state.

[122] D. Gerhard (ed), *Ständische Vertretungen in Europa im 17. und 18. Jahrhundert* (Göttingen, 1969). A classic collection on early modern representative systems.

[123] O. Gierke, *Community in Historical Perspective* [1868] (Cambridge, 1990). An influential theorist on corporations and community-creation.

[124] K. Górski, 'La ligue des Etats et les origines du régime représentatif en Prusse', *Communitas, Princeps, Corona Regni. Studia selecta*. RTNT 87/1 (Warsaw, 1976), 32–41. A Polish voice in the European debate about the origins and function of representative systems.

[125] O. Hintze, 'The Hohenzollern and the Nobility', F. Gilbert (ed., assisted by R.M. Berdahl), *The Historical Essays of Otto Hintze* (Oxford, 1975), 43–63. A classic study of the dualism between ruler and estates.

[126] A. Kamieński, 'Das Ringen der Stände von Kleve-Mark mit den absolutistischen Bestrebungen des Grossen Kurfürsten', *Forschungen zur Brandenburgischen und Preussischen Geschichte* NF 3 (1993), 147–66, traces the Cleves estates' resistance to the Elector's policies.

[127] A. Kamieński, *Stany Prus Książęcych wobec rządów brandenburskich w drugiej połowie XVII wieku* (Olsztyn, 1995). Influential archival study based on the dualist model of Prussian estates versus the Great Elector.

[128] H.G. Koenigsberger (ed.), *Republiken und Republikanismus im Europa der Frühen Neuzeit*. Schriften des Historischen Kollegs Kolloquien 11 (Munich, 1988).

[129] J. Kunisch, 'Die deutschen Führungsschichten im Zeitalter des Absolutismus', H.H. Hofmann und G. Franz (eds), *Deutsche Führungsschichten in der Neuzeit* (Boppard, 1980), 111–41.

[130] W. Neugebauer, *Standschaft als Verfassungproblem. Die historischen Grundlagen ständischer Partizipation in ostmitteleuropäischen Regionen* (Goldbach, 1995). Argues for the need to include Prussia in a comparison of east-central European estate societies.

[131] W. Neugebauer, *Neumärkische Stände* (Rep. 23 B) introd. M. Beck (Frankfurt/M., 2000), provides a detailed study of the activities of the Neumark estates.

[132] W. Neugebauer, 'Adelsständische Tradition und absolutistische Herrschaft. Zur politischen Kultur Westpreußens nach 1772', *Nordost-Archiv. Zeitschrift für Regionalgeschichte* NF VI/2 (1997), 629–47, argues

in favour of the 'permanence of the estates' in eighteenth-century West Prussia. Part of a polemic with [36].

[133] W. Neugebauer, 'Zwischen Preußen und Rußland. Rußland, Ostpreußen und die Stände im Siebenjährigen Krieg', E. Hellmuth, et al. (eds), *Zeitenwende? Preußen um 1800* (Stuttgart, 1999), 43–76, examines the role of the estates during the Seven Years War.

[134] E. Opgenoorth, 'Politische Prozesse unter Kurfürst Friedrich Wilhelm. Eine Studie über Macht und Recht im Absolutismus', *Forschungen zur Brandenburgischen und Preussischen Geschichte* NF 18/2 (2008), 135–52. By the author of the most detailed biography of the Great Elector to date.

[135] J. Paczkowski,'Der Große Kurfürst und Christian Ludwig von Kalckstein', *Forschungen zur Brandenburgischen und Preußischen Geschichte* 2 (1889), 103–209, stresses the estates' resistance against the Elector's policies towards Poland.

[136] S. Pufendorf (J. Tully, ed., M. Silverthrone, trans.), *On the Duty of Man and Citizen*. Cambridge Texts in the History of Political Thought (Cambridge, 1991).

[137] H. Rachel, *Der Grosse Kurfürst und die ostpreußischen Stände 1640–1688* (Leipzig, 1909). A classic study of the Great Elector's policies in Ducal Prussia.

[138] M. Schaupp, *Die Landstände in den zollerischen Fürstentümern Ansbach und Kulmbach im 16. Jahrhundert* (Munich, 2004). A study of the Franconian estates.

[139] A. Seraphim, 'Eine politische Denkschrift des Burggrafen Fabian von Dohna (1606)', *Forschungen zur Brandenburgischen und Preußischen Geschichte* 24 (1911), 109–46.

[140] Q. Skinner, M. van Gelderen (eds), *Republicanism: A Shared European Heritage*, 2 vols, I (Cambridge 2002), esp. articles by Friedeburg, Opaliński and van Gelderen.

[141] B. Stollberg-Rilinger, *Vormünder des Volkes? Konzepte landständischer Repräsentation in der Spätphase des Alten Reiches*. Historische Forschungen 64 (Berlin, 1999), studies the political theory of representation in Enlightenment Germany.

[142] B. Stollberg-Rilinger, 'Vom Volk übertragene Rechte? Zur naturrechtlichen Umdeutung ständischer Verfassungsstrukturen im 18. Jahrhundert', D. Klippel (ed.), *Naturrecht und Staat. Politische Funktionen des europäischen Naturrechts* (Munich, 2006), 103–18.

[143] B. Stollberg-Rilinger (ed.), *Politisch-soziale Praxis und symbolische Kultur der landständischen Verfassungen im westfälischen Raum*. Westfälische Forschungen 53 (2003). Ponders on the power of political symbolism used by the Westphalian estates; esp. the introduction and the article by Kaiser on the estates of Cleves/Mark.

Religion, Reformation and the Problem of Toleration

[144] A. Ajzensztejn, *Die jüdische Gemeinschaft in Königsberg. Von der Niederlassung bis zur rechtlichen Gleichstellung* (Hamburg, 2004).

Select Bibliography

[145] O. Becher, *Herrschaft und autonome Konfessionalisierung. Politik, Religion und Modernisierung in der frühneuzeitlichen Grafschaft Mark* (Essen, 2006), probes the limits of confessionalisation by the state.

[146] H.-W. Bergerhausen, *Friedensrecht und Toleranz. Zur Politik des preußischen Staates gegenüber der katholischen Kirche in Schlesien 1740–1806* (Berlin, 1999), demonstrates that Prussian confessional policies in Silesia were limited by diplomatic relations and other pragmatic considerations.

[147] P. Blickle, *From the Communal Reformation to the Revolution of the Common Man* (Leiden, 1998), formulates the concept of the 'Reformation of the Common Man'.

[148] P. Blickle, *Von der Leibeigenschaft zu den Menschenrechten. Eine Geschichte der Freiheit*, 2nd ed. (München, 2006).

[149] H.-J. Bömelburg, 'Lojalność w protestancko-kalwińskiej rodzinie stanu panów w Prusach Książęcych: trzy pokolenia rodziny Dohnów (1540–1625)', J. Axer (ed.), *Panorama Lojalności. Prusy Królewskie i Prusy Książęce w XVI wieku* (Warsaw, 2001), 46–62, analyses the pro-Calvinist course of one of Prussia's most eminent noble families.

[150] A. Bruer, *Geschichte der Juden in Preußen (1750–1820)* (Frankfurt/M., New York, 1991).

[151] C. M. Clark, *The Politics of Conversion: Missionary Protestantism and the Jews in Prussia 1728–1941* (Oxford, 1995).

[152] C. Clark, 'Piety, politics and society: Pietism in eighteenth-century Prussia', [5], 68–107.

[153] M. Fulbrook, *Piety and Politics: Religion and the Rise of Absolutism in England, Württemberg and Prussia* (Cambridge, 1983). Comparative study of European Pietist movements.

[154] R. L. Gawthrop, *Pietism and the Making of Eighteenth-Century Prussia* (Cambridge, 1993). Links Pietism to the idea of the German *Sonderweg*.

[155] P. S. Gorski, *The Disciplinary Revolution: Calvinism and the Rise of the State in Early Modern Europe* (Chicago, 2003). A sociologist's view of confessionalisation.

[156] F. Hartweg, S. Jersch-Wenzel (eds), *Die Hugenotten und das Refuge: Deutschland und Europa* (Berlin, 1990), esp. the articles by Birnstiel and Klingenbiel.

[157] J.M. Headley et al. (eds), *Confessionalization in Europe, 1555–1700: Essays in Honor and Memory of Bodo Nischan* (Farnham, 2004).

[158] G. Heinrich, 'Religionstoleranz in Brandenburg-Preußen. Idee und Wirklichkeit', M. Schlenke (ed.), *Preußen. Politik, Kultur, Gesellschaft*, 2 vols, I (Hamburg, 1986), 83–102.

[159] C. Hinrichs, *Preußentum und Pietismus. Der Pietismus in Brandenburg-Preußen als religiös-soziale Bewegung* (Göttingen, 1971). Still the most authoritative study on Prussian Pietism.

[160] O. Hintze, 'Die Epochen des evangelischen Kirchenregiments in Preußen', O. Hintze (ed. G. Oestreich), *Regierung und Verwaltung. Gesammelte Abhandlungen zur Staats-, Rechts- und Sozialgeschichte Preußens* (Göttingen, 1967), 56–96.

Select Bibliography

[161] S. Jersch-Wenzel, *Juden und 'Franzosen' in der Wirtschaft des Raumes Berlin/Brandenburg zur Zeit des Merkantilismus* (Berlin, 1978). Draws interesting parallels between policies involving these two groups.

[162] M. Kohnke, 'Geschichte der jüdischen Gemeinde in Biesenthal von ihrer Gründung bis zur Auflösung im Jahre 1758', *Jahrbuch für Brandenburgische Landesgeschichte* 53 (2002), 90–121. Study of a distinct Prussian Jewish community.

[163] M. Lehmann, *Preußen und die katholische Kirche seit 1640*, 7 vols (Leipzig 1878–94), II, no. 218. Collection of primary sources documenting the role of Catholicism in Prussia.

[164] B. Marschke, *Absolutely Pietist: Patronage, Factionalism, and State-Building in the Early Eighteenth-Century Prussian Army Chaplaincy* (Tübingen, 2005), analyses Pietism as a patronage network.

[165] H.-J. Müller, *Irenik als Kommunikationsreform. Das Colloqium Charitativum in Thorn 1645* (Göttingen, 2003), studies irenicism as 'debate culture' during the last religious colloquium designed to safeguard Protestantism in Poland.

[166] B. Nischan, *Prince, People and Confession: The Second Reformation in Brandenburg* (Philadelphia, 1994). A comprehensive study of the success and failure of Calvinist confessionalisation in Brandenburg.

[167] B. Nischan, *Lutherans and Calvinists in the Age of Confessionalism* (Aldershot, 1999), 155–73. A collection of his articles.

[168] V. Press, 'Außerhalb des Religionsfriedens? Das reformierte Bekenntnis im Reich bis 1648', G. Vogler (ed.), *Wegscheiden der Reformation. Alternatives Denken vom 16. bis zum 18. Jahrhundert* (Weimar, 1994), 309–35, considers the situation of the Calvinists in the Empire before 1648.

[169] W. Reinhard, 'Reformation, Counter-Reformation and the Early Modern State: A Reassessment', *Catholic Historical Review* 75 (1989), 383–404. Helped reformulating the concept of 'Counter-Reformation' into 'Catholic Confessionalisation'.

[170] M. Rudersdorf, 'Patriarchalisches Fürstenregiment und Reichsfriede. Zur Rolle des neuen lutherischen Regententyps im Zeitalter der Konfessionalisierung', H. Duchhardt, M. Schnettger (eds), *Reichsständische Libertät und Habsburgisches Kaisertum* (Mainz, 1999), 309–27.

[171] T. Schenk, 'Der preussische Weg der Judenemanzipation: Zur Judenpolitik des "aufgeklärten Absolutismus"', *Zeitschrift für Historische Forschung* 35/3 (2008), 449–82.

[172] H. Schilling, *Religion, Political Culture and the Emergence of Early Modern Society* (Leiden: Brill, 1992), develops Zeeden's concept of 'formation of confessions' into the paradigm of 'confessionalisation'; see [175].

[173] M. Walker, *The Salzburg Transaction: Expulsion and Redemption in Eighteenth-Century Germany* (Ithaca, 1992).

[174] J. Wijaczka, *Stosunki polsko-niemieckie w XVI–XVIII wieku* (Kielce, 2002), esp. the article by Bömelburg.

[175] E.W. Zeeden, *Konfessionsbildung. Studien zur Reformation, Gegenreformation und katholischen Reform* (Stuttgart, 1985). Gave first impulses for the concept of confessionalisation.

Select Bibliography

[176] W. Ziegler, A. Schindling (eds), *Die Territorien des Reichs im Zeitalter der Reformation und Konfessionalisierung. Land und Konfession 1500–1650* (Münster, 1997). Useful survey of territorial confessionalisation in the Empire.

The Rural Economy and Power Relations on the Land

[177] T.H. Aston and C.H.E. Philipin (eds), *The Brenner Debate* (Cambridge, 1985), esp. article by Wunder. Sets out the stereotypical image of serfdom which is challenged by Hagen and Peters.
[178] R. M. Berdahl, *The Politics of the Prussian Nobility: The Development of a Conservative Ideology, 1770–1848* (Princeton, NJ, 1988), presents a picture of peasant oppression.
[179] F. L. Carsten, *A History of the Prussian Junkers* (Aldershot, 1989), challenges older views of absolutism.
[180] M. Countess Dönhoff, *Entstehung und Bewirtschaftung eines ostelbischen Großbetriebs. Die Friedrichsteiner Güter von der Ordenszeit bis zur Bauernbefreiung* (Basel, 1935). A youthful attempt to research her family's social and economic history.
[181] L. Enders, 'Die Landgemeinde in Brandenburg. Grundzüge ihrer Funktion und Wirkunsweise vom 13. bis zum 18. Jahrhundert', *Blätter für deutsche Landesgeschichte*, NF 129 (1993), 195–256.
[182] F. Göse, *Rittergut – Garnison – Residenz. Studien zur Sozialstruktur und politischen Wirksamkeit des brandenburgischen Adels 1648–1763* (Berlin, 2005). Representative of a new social history of the Brandenburg-Prussian nobility.
[183] P. Guzowski, 'Sytuajca ekonomiczna chłopów polskich w XV i XVI w. na tle europejskim', J. Wijaczka, J. Dumanowski (eds), *Życie gospodarcze Rzeczypospolitej w XVI–XVIII wieku. Materiały konferencji naukowej. Między Zachodem a Wschodem*, vol. V (Toruń, 2007) summarises new approaches to serfdom in Poland.
[184] W.W. Hagen, *Ordinary Prussians: Brandenburg Junkers and Villagers, 1500–1840* (Cambridge, 2002). Meticulous archival work on a Brandenburg estate through the centuries, querying previous assumptions about East Elbian Gutsherrschaft.
[185] W.W. Hagen, 'Seventeenth-Century Crisis in Brandenburg: The Thirty Years' War, the Destabilization of Serfdom and the Rise of Absolutism', *American Historical Review* 94 (1989), 302–35.
[186] H. Kaak, *Die Gutsherrschaft. Theoriegeschichtliche Untersuchungen zum Agrarwesen im ostelbischen Raum*. Veröffentlichungen der Historischen Kommission zu Berlin 79 (Berlin, 1991).
[187] W. Kula, *An Economic Theory of the Feudal System: Towards a Model of the Polish Economy, 1500–1800* (London, 1976). Influential post-Stalinist Marxist approach to feudal economy.
[188] E. Melton, 'Gutsherrschaft in East Elbian Germany and Livonia, 1500–1800: A Critique of the Model', *Central European History*, 21/4 (1988), 315–49.

Select Bibliography

[189] C. Motsch, *Grenzgesellschaft und frühmoderner Staat. Die Starostei Draheim zwischen Hinterpommern, der Neumark und Großpolen (1575–1805)* (Göttingen, 2001).

[190] W. Neugebauer, R. Pröve (eds), *Agrarische Verfassung und politische Struktur. Studien zur Gesellschaftsgeschichte Preußens, 1700–1918* (Berlin, 1998), esp. article by R. Schiller on Frederick II's noble protection policies.

[191] W. Neugebauer, 'Zur Geschichte des preußischen Untertanen, besonders im 18. Jahrhundert', *Forschungen zur Brandenburgischen und Preussischen Geschichte* N.F. 13/2 (2003), 141–61.

[192] M. North, *From the North Sea to the Baltic: Essays in Commercial, Monetary and Agricultural History, 1500–1800* (Aldershot, 1996).

[193] J. Peters (ed. with A. Lubinski), *Gutsherrschaft als soziales Modell: vergleichende Betrachtungen zur Funktionsweise frühneuzeitlicher Agrargesellschaften*. Historische Zeitschrift, Beiheft N.F. 18 (1995), 3–21, esp. the introduction by Peters. Path-breaking social research on the previously neglected topic of everyday life in East Elbian Germany.

[194] J. Peters (ed. with A. Lubinski), *Gutsherrschaftsgesellschaften im europäischen Vergleich* (Berlin, 1997), esp. article by Hagen.

[195] J. Peters, B. Krug-Richter (eds), *Konflikt und Kontrolle in Gutherrschaftsgesellschaften: über Resistenz- und Herrschaftsverhalten in ländlichen Sozialgebilden der Frühen Neuzeit* (Göttingen, 1995). Archive-based studies on peasant resistance, revising the image of the oppressed, passive rural subject, esp. article by Enders.

[196] H. Plehn, 'Zur Geschichte der Agrarverfassung von Ost- und Westpreußen', *Forschungen zur Brandenburgischen Geschichte* 17 (1904), 383–466. Still a valuable study of Prussia's rural constitution.

[197] R. Pröve, B. Kölling (eds), *Leben und Arbeiten auf märkischem Sand. Wege in die Gesellschaftsgeschichte Brandenburgs 1700–1914* (Bielefeld, 1999). Excellent collection of new social history.

[198] C. Schmidt, *Leibeigenschaft im Ostseeraum. Versuch einer Typologie* (Köln, 1997). Useful survey, but rather superficial comparison of serfdom in the Baltic.

[199] T. Scott (ed.), *The Peasantries of Europe: From the Fourteenth to the Eighteenth Centuries* (London, New York, 1998), esp. the article by Hagen.

[200] Z. Szultka, 'Znaczenie Akademii Rycerskiej w Kołobrzegu w procesie przeobrażeń szlachty Pomorza Brandenbursko-Pruskiego w drugiej połowie XVII i w początkach XVIII w.', *Rocznik Koszaliński* 1982, 75–99. A useful analysis of the role and impact of noble education and political values in Pomerania.

[201] H. Wunder, 'Aspekte der Gutsherrschaft im Herzogtum und Königreich Preußen im 17. und zu Beginn des 18. Jahrhunderts. Das Beispiel Dohna', in [194], 225–50, analyses moral and religious motivations of noble economic policies.

Cities and Urban Economy

[202] A. Achremczyk, 'Związek małych miast Prus Królewskich, 1683–1772', *Zapiski Historyczne* 44 (1979), 25–45.

Select Bibliography

[203] P. Blickle (ed.), *Landgemeinde und Stadtgemeinde in Mitteleuropa*. Historische Zeitschrift, Beiheft 13 (1991), esp. article by Blickle on communalism as heuristic concept and Engel on the communal character of Brandenburg towns.

[204] K. Friedrich, 'The development of the Prussian town, 1720–1815', in [5], 129–50.

[205] J. Jasiński, *Historia Królewca* (Olsztyn, 1994). On Königsberg's relations to Polish culture.

[206] H. Marti, M. Komorowski (eds), *Die Universität Königsberg in der Frühen Neuzeit* (Köln, Weimar, Wien, 2008), covers a wide spectrum of university activities, scholars and disciplines.

[207] B. Meier, 'Bürgertum und Stadteliten im 18. Jahrhundert. Das Beispiel der Mark Brandenburg', in R. Eßer, T. Fuchs, *Kulturmetropolen – Metropolenkultur. Die Stadt als Kommunikationsraum im 18. Jahrhundert* (Berlin, 2002), 59–79, on Brandenburg's cities as 'spaces of cultural communication'.

[208] O. Mörke , 'Der gewollte Weg in Richtung "Untertan". Ökonomische und politische Eliten in Braunschweig, Lüneburg und Göttingen vom 15. bis zum 17. Jahrhundert', H. Schilling, H. Dideriks (eds), *Bürgerliche Eliten in den Niederlanden und Nordostdeutschland* (Cologne, 1985), 111–133. Comparative study of urban elites.

[209] W. Neugebauer, 'Staatsverwaltung, Manufaktur und Garnison. Die polyfunktionale Residenzlandschaft von Berlin-Potsdam-Wusterhausen zur Zeit Friedrich Wilhelms I.', *Forschungen zur Brandenburgischen und Preußischen Geschichte* N.F. 7/2 (1997), 235–57. Stresses the polyfunctional role of Berlin and Potsdam.

[210] W. Neugebauer, 'Potsdam – Berlin. Zur Behördentopographie des preußischen Absolutismus', B. Kroener, H. Ostertag (eds), *Potsdam. Staat, Armee, Residenz in der preußisch-deutschen Militärgeschichte* (Frankfurt/M., 1993), 273–96.

[211] F. Nicolai, *Beschreibung der Königlichen Residenzstädte Berlin und Potsdam aller daselbst befindlicher Merkwürdigkeiten und der umliegenden Gegend* [1769]. 3 vols, vol I (Berlin, 1786). Description of Berlin by one of the luminaries of the Berlin Enlightenment.

[212] G. Schmoller, 'Das Städtewesen unter Friedrich Wilhelm I', *Zeitschrift für Preußische Geschichte und Landeskunde* 11 (1874), 513–82.

[213] H. Schultz, *Handwerker, Kaufleute, Bankiers. Wirtschaftsgeschichte Europas 1500–1800* (Frankfurt/Main, 1997). Valuable textbook on European economic history.

[214] H. Schultz, *Der Roggenpreis und die Kriege des großen Königs. Chronik und Rezeptsammlung des Berliner Bäckermeisters Johann Friedrich Heyde 1740 bis 1786* (Berlin, 1988), presents a fascinating source on Berlin's commercial population.

[215] K. Vetter, *Zwischen Dorf und Stadt – Die Mediatstädte des Kurmärkischen Kreises Lebus* (Weimar 1996). Focuses on noble and excise towns.

[216] A. Winter, *Das Gelehrtenschulwesen der Residenzstadt Berlin in der Zeit von Konfessionalisierung, Pietismus und Frühaufklärung, 1574–1740* (Berlin, 2008) A rather descriptive approach to religious and Pietist education in Berlin.

Select Bibliography

[217] J. Ziekursch, *Das Ergebnis der Friderizianischen Städteverwaltung und die Städteordnung Steins, am Beispiel der schlesischen Städte dargestellt* (Jena, 1908). One of the few older works that avoids idealising the impact of Frederick II's invasion of Silesia.

Monarchy (from 1701), Monarchs and the Court

[218] P. Bahners, G. Roellecke (eds), *Preußische Stile. Ein Staat als Kunststück* (Stuttgart, 2001), esp. articles by Vec and Hahn on the ceremonial politics of the new Prussian monarchy.

[219] H. Barmeyer, *Die preußische Rangerhöhung und Königskrönung 1701 in deutscher und europäischer Sicht* (Frankfurt/M., 2002), esp. articles by Weiss and Körber.

[220] P. Baumgart, 'Der deutsche Hof der Barockzeit als politische Institution', A. Buck (ed.), *Europäische Hofkultur im 16. und 17. Jahrhundert*. Wolfenbütteler Arbeitskreis zur Barockforschung 9 (Hamburg, 1981), 25–43.

[221] J. J. Berns, T. Rahn (eds), *Zeremoniell als höfische Ästhetik in Spätmittelalter und früher Neuzeit* (Tübingen, 1995), 57–73, esp. article by Gestrich.

[222] J. von Besser, *Preußische Krönungs-Geschichte/oder Verlauf der Zeremonien* (Cölln an der Spree, 1702). Famous work by Frederick's master of ceremonies.

[223] F. Brunn (ed.), Frédéric, Roi de Prusse, *Mémoires pour servir a l'histoire des quatre derniers souverains de la maison de Brandenbourg* (Berlin, 1791). Frederick's writings on the past and future of his dynasty.

[224] A. Bues, I. Kąkolewski (eds), *Die Testamente Herzog Albrechts von Preußen aus den sechziger Jahren des 16. Jahrhunderts* (Wiesbaden, 1999). Edition of Duke Albrecht's testaments.

[225] R. Dietrich (ed.), *Die Politischen Testamente der Hohenzollern* (Cologne, Vienna, 1986). Collection of the Hohenzollerns' political testaments.

[226] R. Ergang, *The Potsdam Führer: Frederick William I, Father of Prussian Militarism* (New York, 1941). Readers must take the context of 1941 into account.

[227] K. Friedrich, S. Smart, *The Cultivation of Monarchy and the Rise of Berlin: Brandenburg-Prussia 1700* (Farnham, 2010). Analysis of the coronation of 1701, supported by edited and annotated documents.

[228] A. Gestrich, *Absolutismus und Öffentlichkeit. Politische Kommunikation in Deutschland zu Beginn des 18. Jahrhunderts* (Göttingen, 1994). Influential work on communication and the Enlightenment public sphere.

[229] P.M. Hahn, H. Lorenz (eds), *Pracht und Herrlichkeit: Adelig-fürstliche Lebensstile im 17. und 18. Jahrhundert* (Potsdam, 1998), esp. article by Hahn on popular perceptions of court culture.

[230] O. Hauser (ed.), *Friedrich der Große in seiner Zeit* (Cologne, Vienna, 1987). Traditional, positive evaluation of Frederick II in a wider context, albeit excluding his relationship to Poland.

Select Bibliography

[231] M. Hein, 'Preußische Hofordnungen des 16. Jahrhunderts', *Altpreußische Forschungen* 1 (1925), 52–68.

[232] E. Hellmuth, 'Die "Wiedergeburt" Friedrichs des Großen und der "Tod fürs Vaterland". Zum patriotischen Selbstverständnis in Preußen in der zweiten Hälfte des 18. Jahrhunderts', E. Hellmuth, R. Stauber (eds), *Nationalismus vor dem Nationalismus?* Aufklärung 10, Beiheft 2 (Hamburg, 1998), 23–54.

[233] E. Hinrichs, 'Die Königskrönung vom 18. Januar 1701 – ein historiographisches und ein historisches Problem', Matthias Weber (ed.), *Preussen in Ostmitteleuropa. Geschehensgeschichte und Verstehensgeschichte* (Oldenburg, 2003), 35–61. Interesting volume on Prussia's east-central European context.

[234] O. Hintze, *Die Hohenzollern und ihr Werk: 500 Jahre vaterländische Geschichte* (Berlin, 1915). Echoes the classic, ruler-focused view of Borussian historiography.

[235] W. Hubatsch, *Frederick the Great: Absolutism and Administration* (London, 1973). Traditional praise for the king.

[236] R. Koser, H. Droysen (eds), *Briefwechsel Friedrichs des Großen mit Voltaire*, 3 vols (Leipzig 1908–11), here III.

[237] J. Kunisch, *Friedrich der Grosse. Der König und seine Zeit* (Munich, 2004). A differentiated yet positive evaluation of Frederick II.

[238] J. Kunisch (ed.), *Dreihundert Jahre Preußische Königskrönung. Eine Tagungsdokumentation*. Forschungen zur Brandenburgischen und Preußischen Geschichte N.F. Beiheft 6 (Berlin, 2002), esp. articles by Stollberg-Rilinger, Plassmann and Roll on the ramifications of the 1701 Prussian coronation.

[239] D. McKay, *The Great Elector: Profiles in Power* (Harlow, 2001). A most valuable political biography.

[240] I. Mittenzwei, *Friedrich II von Preußen* (Berlin [East], 1987). Reflects a former East German historian's dilemma of having to condemn a 'feudal ruler' and being proud of aspects of the Prussian heritage that agree with a socialist approach.

[241] W. Neugebauer, *Residenz – Verwaltung – Repräsentation. Das Berliner Schloß und seine historischen Funktionen vom 15. bis zum 20. Jahrhundert* (Potsdam, 1999).

[242] W. Neugebauer, 'Friedrich III./I. (1688–1713)', F.-L. Kroll (ed.), *Preussens Herrscher. Von den ersten Hohenzollern bis Wilhelm II.* (Munich, 2000), 113–33, revises the negative older view of the king.

[243] W. Neugebauer, 'Residenzpraxis und Politik in Kurbrandenburg im 16. Jahrhundert', *Jahrbuch für brandenburgische Landesgeschichte* 51 (2000), 124–38.

[244] H.-J. Neumann, *Friedrich Wilhelm II. Preußen unter den Rosenkreuzern* (Berlin, 1997). Subtle discussion of the 'anti-enlightened' character of Frederick William II's reign.

[245] B. Meier, *Friedrich Wilhelm II. – König von Preußen (1744–1797). Ein Leben zwischen Rokoko und Revolution* (Regensburg, 2007). Shows that most Prussian kings had trouble with their successors; revises the king's older negative image.

Select Bibliography

[246] Lord Plantamour, 'Letters from Lord Plantamour, envoy to Berlin, to Blathwayt' (1701), Manuscript, British Library Egerton MSS 2428, f. 13v.

[247] V. Press, 'Friedrich der Große als Reichspolitiker', H. Duchhardt (ed.), *Friedrich der Grosse, Franken und das Reich* (Köln, 1986), 25–56. Examines Frederick II's role in imperial politics.

[248] W. Ribbe (ed.), *Schloß und Schloßbezirk* (Berlin, 2005), esp. chapters by Hinterkeuser and Neugebauer on the changing role of the royal residences.

[249] G. Ritter (trans. P. Paret), *Frederick the Great* (Berkeley, 1968).

[250] S. Salmonowicz, *Fryderyk II* (Wrocław, 1981). A critical but balanced portrait.

[251] B. Stollberg-Rilinger, 'Höfische Öffentlichkeit. Zur zeremoniellen Selbstdarstellung des brandenburgischen Hofes vor dem europäischen Publikum', *Forschungen zur Brandenburgischen und Preußischen Geschichte* N.F. 7 (1997), 145–76, analyses the coronation through the lense of a cultural history of political communication.

[252] B. Stollberg-Rilinger, 'Zeremoniell als politisches Verfahren: Rangordnung und Rangstreit als Strukturmerkmale des frühmodernen Reichstags', J. Kunisch (ed.), *Neue Studien zur frühneuzeitlichen Rechtsgeschichte*. Zeitschrift für Historische Forschung, Beiheft 19 (Berlin, 1997), 91–132.

[253] B. Szymczak, *Fryderyk Wilhelm. Wielki Elektor* (Wrocław, Warsaw, 2006). A synthesis of Polish research on the Elector's policies towards Poland.

[254] J. Toland, *An Account of the Courts of Prussia and Hanover, sent to a Minister of State in Holland by J.T.* (London, 1705). A republican praising German monarchy for the sake of the Protestant succession.

[255] H. Watanabe O'Kelly, *Court Culture in Early Modern Dresden* (Houndmills, 2002).

[256] F. Windt et al. (eds), *Preußen 1701: Eine europäische Geschichte*. 2 vols, I: *Essays. Katalog der Ausstellung in der Großen Orangerie des Schlosses Charlottenburg 6. Mai bis 5. August 2001* (Berlin, 2001), esp. article by Schubersky. Luxurious publication for the anniversary of the Prussian coronation, with much new material.

[257] V. Wittenauer, *Im Dienste der Macht: Kultur und Sprache am Hof der Hohenzollern. Vom Großen Kurfürsten zu Wilhelm II.* (Paderborn, 2007), analyses the influence of French culture and language on the Prussian court.

Foreign Policy and International Relations

[258] P. Baumgart, 'Die preußische Königserhebung von 1701, König August II. und die polnische Republik', *Jahrbuch für Geschichte Mittel- und Ostdeutschlands* 47 (2001), 23–48.

[259] F. Bostel, 'Przeniesienie Lenna Pruskiego na Elektorów Brandenburskich', *Przewodnik Naukowy i Literacki* 9/6 (Lwów, 1883), 557–72. Sees the partitions rooted in Poland's failure to incorporate Prussia in the sixteenth century.

Select Bibliography

[260] T. Cegielski, 'Preussische "Deutschland – und Polenpolitik" in dem Zeitraum 1740–1792', *Jahrbuch für die Geschichte Mittel- und Ostdeutschlands* 30 (1981), 21–7. Provides valuable background on Prussia's role in the partitions.

[261] W. Czapliński, *Polska, Prusy i Brandenburgia* (Wrocław, 1947). A classic work which supports Polish claims to Ducal Prussia within the context of post-war Poland's shift to the West.

[262] S. and H. Dolezel (eds), *Die Staatsverträge des Herzogtums Preussen. Part I: Polen und Litauen. Verträge und Belehnungsurkunden 1525–1657/58* (Berlin, 1971). Collection of political treatises concluded by Ducal Prussia with Poland.

[263] S. Dolezel, *Das preußisch-polnische Lehnsverhältnis unter Herzog Albrecht von Preußen* (Cologne, 1967), analyses the relationship between Poland and Prussia in 1525–68.

[264] M. Drozdowski, 'Eighteenth-century Sources of Polish-Prussian Antagonism', *Polish Western Affairs* 22/1–2 (1981), 40–55.

[265] H. Duchhardt, B. Wachowiak, *Um die Souveränität des Herzogtums Preußen. Der Vertrag von Wehlau 1657*. Deutsche und Polen – Geschichte einer Nachbarschaft, part B 5, vol. 82 (Hanover, 1998). Textbook containing annotated primary sources.

[266] E. Hassinger, *Brandenburg-Preußen, Rußland und Schweden, 1700–1713* (Munich, 1953). One of the few studies which focus on the northeastern context of Brandenburg-Prussia's policies.

[267] O. Hauser (ed.), *Preußen, Europa und das Reich*. Neue Forschungen zur Brandenburg-Preussischen Geschichte 7 (Cologne, 1987), esp. article by Schindling and Opgenoorth on the role of the Electorate in the Empire.

[268] A. Kamińska, *Brandenburg-Prussia and Poland-Lithuania: A Study in Diplomatic History (1669–1672)* (Marburg/Lahn, 1983).

[269] U. Kober, *Eine Karriere im Krieg. Graf Adam von Schwarzenberg und die kurbrandenburgische Politik von 1619 bis 1641* (Berlin, 2004). A political biography of the influential Catholic politician at the Brandenburg court.

[270] W. Konopczyński, *Fryderyk Wielki a Polska* (Poznań, 1947). Still the most influential work in Polish on Frederick II's relations with Poland.

[271] H. a Lapide [Chemnitz], *Dissertatio de ratione status in imperio Romano-Germanico* (Freistadt, 1647), describes the Empire as ruled by an aristocracy.

[272] L. R. Lewitter, 'Russia, Poland and the Baltic, 1697–1721', *Historical Journal* XI/1 (1968), 3–34.

[273] J. Lukowski, *The Partitions of Poland: 1772, 1793, 1795* (Harlow, 1999). A valuable survey of the political background of the three partitions.

[274] D. Makiłła, *Między Welawą a Królewcem 1657–1701. Geneza Królestwa w Prusach (Königtum in Preußen). Studium historyczno-prawne* (Toruń, 1998). Puts the Polish–Prussian treaties and the coronation to a constitutional test.

[275] J. Małłek, *Preussen und Polen. Politik, Stände, Kirche und Kultur vom 16. bis zum 18. Jahrhundert* (Stuttgart, 1992). Articles on the relationship between Royal and Ducal Prussia.

Select Bibliography

[276] K. Marx (ed. W. Conze), *Manuskripte über die polnische Frage* [1863–64] ('s-Gravenhage, 1961).

[277] W. Mediger, *Moskaus Weg nach Europa. Der Aufstieg Rußlands zum europäischen Machtstaat im Zeitalter Friedrichs des Großen* (Braunschweig, 1952). Diplomatic and political history that traces Russia's rise in the age of Frederick II.

[278] T. Moerner (ed.), *Kurbrandenburgs Staatsverträge von 1601 bis 1700* (Berlin, 1867).

[279] M. M. Müller, *Polen zwischen Preußen und Rußland. Staatliche Souveränitätskrise und Reformpolitik, 1736–1752* (Berlin, 1983). Revises the German interpretation that blames the partitions of Poland solely on the Poles.

[280] U. Müller-Weil, *Absolutismus und Aussenpolitik in Preussen. Ein Beitrag zur Strukturgeschichte des preussischen Absolutismus* (Stuttgart, 1992). Champions the primacy of foreign policy.

[281] H. Neuhaus, 'Das Reich im Kampf gegen Friedrich den Großen. Reichsarmee und Reichskriegsführung im Siebenjährigen Krieg', B. Kroener (ed.), *Europa im Zeitalter Friedrichs des Großen. Wirtschaft, Gesellschaft, Kriege* (Munich, 1989), 213–43.

[282] Preußische Akademie der Wissenschaften (ed.), *Politische Correspondenz Friedrichs des Großen*, 46 vols (Berlin, 1879–1939, repr. Osnabrück, 1986), here vol. 32, no. 21.014. Frederick II's political correspondence.

[283] A.F. Pribram, 'Zur auswärtigen Politik des Kurfürsten Friedrich Wilhelm von Brandenburg', *Forschungen zur Brandenburgischen und Preußischen Geschichte* 5 (1892), 103–33.

[284] H.M. Scott, *The Birth of a Great Power System 1740–1815* (Harlow, 2005). A succinct and very useful textbook.

[285] H. M. Scott, 'Prussia's royal foreign minister: Frederick the Great and the administration of Prussian diplomacy', R. Oresko et al. (eds), *Royal and Republican Sovereignty in Early Modern Europe: Essays in Memory of Ragnhild Hatton* (Cambridge, 1997), 500–26.

[286] H.M. Scott, 'Prussia's emergence as a European great power, 1740–1763', in [5], 153–76.

[287] B. Simms, 'The Primate of Foreign Policy', *German History* 21/3 (2003), 275–91.

[288] D. Stievermann, 'Der Fürstenbund von 1785 und das Reich', V. Press (ed.), *Alternativen zur Reichsverfassung in der Frühen Neuzeit?* (Munich, 1995), 209–26.

[289] F. Szabo, *The Seven Years War in Europe, 1756–1763* (Harlow, 2007). A detailed account of the war and its diplomatic consequences.

[290] M. Umbach, 'The politics of sentimentality and the German Fürstenbund, 1779–1785', *Historical Journal* 41 (1998), 679–704.

[291] P.H. Wilson, 'Prussia's relations with the Holy Roman Empire, 1740–1786', *Historical Journal* 51/2 (2008), 337–71, revises the image of Frederick II's Prussia as a power disengaged from the Empire.

[292] K. Zernack, *Nordosteuropa – Skizzen und Beiträge zu einer Geschichte der Ostseeländer* (Lüneburg, 1993). Articles by one of the most influential

scholars on the history of north-east Europe, who contributed much to overcome the limited visions of national history.

[293] K. Zernack, 'Negative Polenpolitik als Grundlage deutsch-russischer Diplomatie in der Mächtepolitik des 18. Jahrhunderts', U. Liszkowski (ed.), *Rußland und Deutschland. Festschrift für Georg von Rauch* (Stuttgart, 1974), 144–59.

[294] K. Zernack 'Das preussische Königtum und die polnische Republik im europäischen Mächtesystem des 18. Jahrhunderts (1701–1763)', *Jahrbuch für die Geschichte Mittel- und Ostdeutschlands* 30 (1981), 4–20.

[295] K. Zernack, 'Polen in der Geschichte Preußens', O. Büsch (ed.), *Handbuch der preussischen Geschichte. II: Das 19. Jahrhundert und Große Themen der Geschichte Preußens* (Berlin, New York, 1992), 377–448, traces the much neglected history of Prussian–Polish relations from harmonious co-operation to hostile occupation.

The Prussian Military and 'Social Militarisation'

[296] O. Büsch (trans. J. Gagliardo), *Military System and Social Life in Old Regime Prussia, 1713–1807: The Beginnings of the Social Militarization of Prusso-German Society* [1967] (Boston, 1997). A highly influential contribution to the *Sonderweg* school, focusing on the Kanton system and the role of the nobility.

[297] R. I. Frost, *After the Deluge. Poland-Lithuania and the Second Northern War 1655–1660* (Cambridge, 1993). Analyses the problems of the Polish monarchy in the mid-seventeenth century.

[298] R.I. Frost, *The Northern Wars, 1558–1721* (Harlow, 2000). A comprehensive treatment of the military, political and social aspects of the Northern Wars.

[299] H. Th. Gräf, 'Militarisierung der Stadt oder Urbanisierung des Militärs? Ein Beitrag zur Militärgeschichte der frühen Neuzeit aus stadtgeschichtlicher Perspektive', in [302], 89–108.

[300] B. Kroener, R. Pröve (eds), *Krieg und Frieden. Militär und Gesellschaft in der Frühen Neuzeit* (Paderborn, 1996). A social history of the military, esp. articles by Kroener on the standing army, Pröve on quartering, and Kloosterhuis on the Kanton system.

[301] U. Marwitz, *Staatsräson und Landesdefension. Untersuchungen zum Kriegswesen des Herzogtums Preußen 1640–1655* (Boppard a. Rhein, 1984).

[302] R. Pröve (ed.), *Klio in Uniform? Probleme und Perspektiven einer modernen Militärgeschichte der Frühen Neuzeit* (Cologne, 1997) Contains innovative approaches to the social and cultural history of the military, esp. contributions by Nowosadtko and Gräf on military–civilian relations.

[303] R. Pröve, 'Zum Verhältnis von Militär und Gesellschaft im Spiegel gewaltsamer Rekrutierungen (1648–1789)', *Zeitschrift für Historische Forschung* 22/2 (1995), 191–223. Good on civil–military relationships.

[304] D. Riches, 'Early modern military reform and the connection between Sweden and Brandenburg-Prussia', *Scandinavian Studies* 77/3 (2005), 348–64.

Select Bibliography

[305] C.J. Rogers (ed.), *The Military Revolution Debate: Readings on the Military Transformation of Early Modern Europe* (Boulder, CO, 1995). Summarises the main issues and approaches to the paradigm of the 'military revolution'.

[306] H. Schmidt, 'Staat und Armee im Zeitalter des "miles perpetuus"', J. Kunisch, *Staatsverfassung und Mächtepolitik. Zur Genese von Staatenkonflikten im Zeitalter des Absolutismus* (Berlin, 1979), 213–48. An account of the origins and impact of the standing army.

[307] D. E. Schowalter, *The Wars of Frederick the Great* (Harlow, 1996).

[308] M. Sikora, *Disziplin und Desertion. Strukturprobleme militärischer Organisation im 18. Jahrhundert* (Berlin, 1996). An innovative social historical study of desertion.

[309] P.H. Wilson, *War, State and Society in Württemberg, 1677–1793* (Cambridge, 1995). Study of one of the more neglected territories of the Holy Roman Empire; useful for a comparison with the Prussian case.

[310] P.H. Wilson, *German Armies: War and German Politics, 1648–1806* (London, 1998).

[311] P.H. Wilson, 'Social Militarization in Eighteenth-Century Germany', *German History* 18/1 (2000), 1–39, undermines Büsch's thesis of the Junker–officer symbiosis and demonstrates the limitations of the Kanton system.

[312] M. Winter, *Untertanengeist durch Militärpflicht? Die preußische Kantonverfassung in brandenburgischen Städten im 18. Jahrhundert* (Bielefeld, 2005), challenges Büsch's work on the Kanton system by presenting new material, particularly from the context of urban society.

Enlightenment and Public Sphere

[313] T. Ahnert, *Religion and the Origins of the German Enlightenment: Faith and the Reform of Learning in the Thought of Christian Thomasius* (Rochester, NY, 2006).

[314] C.B.A. Behrens, *Society, Government and the Enlightenment: The Experiences of Eighteenth-Century France and Prussia* (New York, 1985), denies that 'enlightened absolutism' ever existed and reinforces the idea of a Prussian *Sonderweg*.

[315] T.C.W. Blanning, *The Culture of Power and the Power of Culture: Old Regime Europe 1660–1789* (Oxford, 2002).

[316] G. Birtsch, 'Friedrich Wilhelm I. und die Anfänge der Aufklärung in Brandenburg-Preußen', in [320], 87–102, tries to rescue Frederick William I for the Enlightenment.

[317] T. Biskup, M. Schalenberg (eds), *Selling Berlin. Imagebildung und Stadtmarketing von der preußischen Residenz bis zur Bundeshauptstadt* (Stuttgart, 2008). Collection of articles on the rapid rise of Berlin.

[318] A.M. Brenker, *Aufklärung als Sachzwang. Realpolitik in Breslau im ausgehenden 18. Jahrhundert* (Munich, 2000). Monograph on Breslau's enlightened public sphere.

Select Bibliography

[319] A.M. Brenker, 'Über Aufklärer und Aufklärergesellschaften in Breslau', *Acta Universitatis Wratislaviensis No. 1757. Germanica Wratislaviensia* CXIV (Wrocław 1996), 9–22.

[320] J. Brewer, E. Hellmuth (eds), *Rethinking Leviathan: The Eighteenth-Century State in Britain and Germany* (Oxford, 1999), esp. articles by Birtsch and Vierhaus, focusing on the public sphere and the bureaucracy.

[321] R. Butterwick et al. (eds), *Peripheries of the Enlightenment* (Oxford, 2008). Focuses on neglected areas of the European Enlightenment outside France.

[322] R. Butterwick, 'What is Enlightenment (Oświecenie)? Some Polish Answers, 1765–1820, *Central Europe* 3/1 (2005), 19–37, introduces a series of influential reform-minded thinkers of the Enlightenment in pre- and post-partition Poland.

[323] C. W. Dohm, *Über die bürgerliche Verbesserung der Juden* (Berlin, Stettin, 1781). Highly influential treatise by an enlightened civil servant, suggesting the assimilation of the Prussian Jews.

[324] M. Erlin, *Berlin's Forgotten Future: City, History and Enlightenment in Eighteenth-Century Germany* (Chapel Hill, 2004), provides a history of the Berlin Enlightenment's struggle with provincialism.

[325] P. Gay, *The Enlightenment*, 2 vols (New York, 1966–9). A classic, focusing on the unity of the Enlightenment.

[326] R. Porter, M. Teich (eds), *The Enlightenment in National Context* (Cambridge, 1981). A brief and still useful introduction to the 'national Enlightenments'.

[327] K. Gerlach, 'Der Freimaurer Prinz Heinrich von Preußen', *Forschungen zur Brandenburgischen und Preußischen Geschichte* NF 17/2 (2007), 191–232.

[328] E. Haberkern, *Limitierte Aufklärung. Die protestantische Spätaufklärung in Preußen am Beispiel der Berliner Mittwochsgesellschaft* (Marburg, 2005), focuses on enlightenend societies and clubs in Berlin.

[329] J. Habermas (trans. T. Burger), *The Structured Transformation of the Public Sphere: An Inquiry into a Category of Bourgeois Society* (Cambridge, MA, 1989). An influential book, written in 1969, linking the development of a public sphere to the emergence of capitalist bourgeois society.

[330] H. Hattenhauer (ed.), *Allgemeines Landrecht für die preußischen Staaten von 1794* (Frankfurt/M., 1970). A modern edition of the Prussian law code.

[331] E. Hellmuth (ed.), *The Transformation of Political Culture: England and Germany in the Late Eighteenth Century* (Oxford, 1990), criticises German historians for ignoring the popular Enlightenment and tries to rectify this deficit; esp. articles by Klippel on the concept of liberty and by Bödeker on Enlightenment journals.

[332] I. Hunter, *Rival Enlightenments: Civil and Metaphysical Philosophy in Early Modern Germany* (Cambridge, 2001), with a citation from Pufendorf, *De Jure Naturae* [1672], VII.vi.6.

[333] J. Israel, *Radical Enlightenment: Philosophy and the Making of Modernity, 1650–1750* (Oxford, 2001), dates the 'radical Enlightenment' back to Spinoza.

Select Bibliography

[334] I. Kant, 'An Answer to the Question: What Is Enlightening?', *Essays and treatises on moral, political, and various philosophical subjects*, 2 vols (London, 1798–99), I, 3–14.

[335] L. Kontler, 'Introduction: The Enlightenment in Central Europe?', in B. Trencsényi and M. Kopecek (eds), *Discourses of Collective Identity in Central and Southeast Europe*, 2 vols, I: Late Enlightenment (Budapest, 2006), 33–44.

[336] L. Krieger, *Kings and Philosophers, 1689–1789* (London, 1970), emphasises the positive *Sonderweg* of enlightened absolutism but condemns Prussia's political legacies for modern Germany.

[337] K. Lambrecht, 'Tabelle und Toleranz. Johann Ignaz von Felbigers Reform der Volksschulbildung in Ostmitteleuropa', M. Scheutz et al. (eds), *Orte des Wissens. Jahrbuch der Österreichischen Gesellschaft zur Erforschung des achtzehnten Jahrhunderts* 18–19 (Bochum, 2004), 153–67.

[338] J.M. von Loen, *Gesammelte Kleine Schriften* (Frankfurt-M., Leipzig, 1749–52) 4 parts, I (1749). Writer who entered Prussian state service and commented on Prussia's court and politics.

[339] J. van Horn Melton, *Absolutism and the Eighteenth-Century Origins of Compulsory Schooling in Prussia and Austria* (Cambridge, 1988).

[340] H. Möller, *Aufklärung in Preussen. Der Verleger, Publizist und Geschichtsschreiber Friedrich Nicolai* (Berlin, 1974), studies Nicolai's impact on the public sphere in Berlin.

[341] T. S. Paine, *The Problem of Being Modern or the German Pursuit of Enlightenment from Leibniz to the French Revolution* (Detroit, 1997).

[342] J.G.A. Pocock, 'The Re-description of Enlightenment', P.J. Marshall (ed.), *Proceedings of the British Academy* (Oxford, 2004), 101–18.

[343] P. Reill, *The German Enlightenment and the Rise of Historicism* (Berkeley, CA, 1975). Important study of the link between the Enlightenment and its impact on historical thinking in the nineteenth century.

[344] H. Reiss (ed.), *Kant's Political Writings* (Cambridge, 1970).

[345] R. Riemenschneider (ed.), *Polen und Deutschland im Zeitalter der Aufklärung. Reformen im Bereich des politischen Lebens, der Verfassung und der Bildung* (Braunschweig, 1982), compares Polish and German education policies and other reforms.

[346] M. Sauter, *Visions of the Enlightenment: The Edict on Religion of 1788 and the Politics of the Public Sphere in Eighteenth-Century Prussia* (Leiden, 2009), revises the negative reputation of Wöllner's Religion Edict in the context of the oral and public culture of the Enlightenment.

[347] H. Scholtz (ed.), *Friedrich Gedike: Über Berlin. Briefe 'Von einem Fremden' in der Berlinischen Monatsschrift 1783–1785. Kulturpädagogische Reflexionen aus der Sicht der 'Berliner Aufklärung'* (Berlin, 1987).

[348] D. Sorkin, *Moses Mendelssohn and the Religious Enlightenment* (Berkeley, 1996). On Mendelssohn's significance for the Jewish and Prussian Enlightenment.

[349] D. Sorkin, 'Reclaiming Theology for the Enlightenment: The Case of Siegmund Jacob Baumgarten (1706–1757)', *Central European History* 36/4 (2003), 503–30. A study of irenicism.

Select Bibliography

[350] P. Weber, 'Das Allgemeine Gesetzbuch – ein Corpus Juris Fridericianum?', M. Fontius (ed.), *Friedrich II. und die europäische Aufklärung. Forschungen zur Brandenburgischen und Preussischen Geschichte* NF, Beiheft 4 (Berlin, 1999), 103–11. Articles analysing Frederick II's relationship to the wider context of the European Enlightenment.

[351] D. Willoweit, 'Johann Heinrich Casimir von Carmer und die preußische Justizreform', J. Kunisch (ed.), *Persönlichkeiten im Umkreis Friedrichs des Großen. Forschungen zur Brandenburgischen und Preußischen Geschichte* 9, NF (Berlin, 1988), 153–74, studies the men who became Prussian bureaucrats and law reformers.

[352] C. Wolff, *Vernünftige Gedanken von dem Gesellschafftlichen Leben der Menschen und insonderheit dem gemeinen Wesen zur Beförderung der Glückseligkeit des menschlichen Geschlechts* (Frankfurt, 1721). Prussia's most eminent writer on natural law.

[353] L. Wolff, *Inventing Eastern Europe: The Map of Civilization on the Mind of the Enlightenment* (Stanford, CA, 1994). A cultural history of 'West looks East'.

From Frederick II to the Defeat of 1806/7

[354] Z. Batscha, J. Garber (eds), *Von der ständischen zur bürgerlichen Gesellschaft. Politisch-soziale Theorien im Deutschland der zweiten Hälfte des 18. Jahrhunderts* (Frankfurt/M., 1981). Reflecting changes in the notion of citizenship.

[355] L. Kittstein, *Politik im Zeitalter der Revolution. Untersuchungen zur preußischen Staatlichkeit, 1792–1807* (Stuttgart, 2003), emphasises the Prussian sense of insecurity as major motive for internal and foreign policy-making.

[356] R. Koselleck, *Preußen zwischen Reform und Revolution. Allgemeines Landrecht, Verwaltung und soziale Bewegung von 1791 bis 1848*, 3rd ed. (Stuttgart, 1981). The most influential study on Prussia to date on the transitional period between the Enlightenment and the Revolutions of 1848.

[357] M. Levinger, 'The Prussian Reform Movement and the rise of enlightened nationalism', in [5], 259–77.

[358] F. Meinecke, *The Age of German Liberation, 1795–1815* (Berkeley, CA, 1977).

[359] B. Simms, *The Impact of Napoleon: Prussian High Politics, Foreign Policy and the Crisis of the Executive, 1797–1806* (Cambridge, 1997).

[360] B. Simms, *The Struggle for Mastery in Germany, 1779–1850* (Basingstoke, 1998). Presents arguments for the primacy of foreign politics.

[361] J. Sperber, 'State and Civil Society in Prussia: Thoughts on a New Edition of Reinhart Koselleck's "Preussen zwischen Reform und Revolution"', *Journal of Modern History* 57/2 (1985), 278–96.

Select Bibliography

Miscellaneous

[362] T. Działyński (ed.), *Acta Tomiciana*, 13 vols (Warsaw, 1796–1861), VII, 255. Polish government documents from 1497 to 1572.
[363] A. Goldgar, R.I. Frost (eds), *Institutional Culture in Early Modern Society* (Leiden, 2004). Proceedings of a conference on institutional culture across Europe.
[364] I. Lukšaitė, 'Matthäus Prätorius, ein Geschichtsschreiber der preußischen Kultur', *Deliciae Prussicae oder Preußische Schaubühne/ Prūsijos Idomybės, arba Prūsijos Regykla*, 7 vols, I (Vilnius, 1999). Source edition of Prätorius's works, demonstrating Lithuania's rediscovery of its Prussian past.
[365] T. Mergel, 'Überlegungen zu einer Kulturgeschichte der Politik', *Geschichte und Gesellschaft* 28/4 (2002), 574–606. Important methodological considerations concerning the new cultural history of politics.
[366] M. Meumann, R. Pröve (eds), *Herrschaft in der Frühen Neuzeit.Umrisse eines dynamisch-kommunikativen Prozesses* (Münster, 2004). An excellent collection on the legitimacy and practice of power, with examples from across the Holy Roman Empire, esp. article by Nowosadtko on early modern standing armies.
[367] J. Morrill, 'Thinking about the New British History', D. Armitage (ed.), *British Political Thought in History, Literature and Theory, 1500–1800* (Cambridge, 2006), 23–46, with thoughts on dynastic agglomerates and composite monarchies.

Websites

[368] *Allgemeines Landrecht* (ALR), I Introduction § 22; ALR I, 1 § 2–7; German version on http://www.smixx.de/ra/Links_F-R/PrALR/pralr.html, last accessed 29 Oct. 2010; printed edition, see [329].
[369] Deutsch-polnische Schulbuchkommission, Friedrich Ebert Stiftung, {http://library.fes.de/library/netzquelle/deutsch-polnisch/schulbuch.html} (last accessed 3 Sept. 2010).
[370] J.D.E. Preuss (ed.), *Oeuvres de Frédéric*, 30 vols (Berlin: Decker, 1846–56), vol. 9: 'Essai sur le forme de gouvernement et sur les devoirs des souverains', 229. [My translation] Digital source University Library Trier http://friedrich.uni-trier.de/de/oeuvres/9/221/ (last accessed: 14 Oct. 2010). Useful internet facsimile of Frederick II's works.

Index

Academy of Sciences, *see* Berlin
Agricola, Johann (1494–1566), Protestant Reformer, 37
Akzise (excise tax), 28–9, 48–9, 53, 54, 74–5, 102
Albert Frederick, duke in Prussia (1568–1618), 50, 84, 85
Albrecht Achilles, Elector of Brandenburg (1470–86), 24–5
Albrecht of Hohenzollern-Ansbach, grand master of the Teutonic Order (1511–25), duke in Prussia (1525–1568), 7, 19–21, 24, 28, 36–7, 49–50, 57–8, 68, 84–5
Allgemeines Landrecht (General Law Code, 1794), 63, 108–10, 112–13, 116
allodification of fiefs, 34, 54, 55
Altmark, xviii, 4, 44, 47–8, 56
American Revolution, 116
Amt (*Amtskammer*), 28–30, 31, 46, 51, 55, 56
Andrusovo, truce of (1667), 88
Anna, electress of Brandenburg (1576–1625), 37, 84
Ansbach, margraviate of, 24, 25, 34, 37, 68, 84
army (Brandenburg-Prussian), 29, 30–6, 52, 55, 56, 62, 66, 69, 72, 76, 80, 82, 86–8, 90, 100–1, 114
  financing, 33, 49, 62, 65, 86
  garrisons, 62, 73–7
  Lange Kerle (tall elite guard), 71
  military jurisdiction, 76
  recruitment, 30–4, 41 60, 86, 92, 100–1, 102

standing army, 22, 24, 32–3, 54, 65, 81, 86, 100
  see also General War Commissariat; *Kanton* system
Augustus II, the 'Strong', elector of Saxony (1694–1733), king of Poland (1697–1706, 1709–1733), 65, 90
Augustus III, elector of Saxony (1733–63), king of Poland (1734–63), 90
Austria, xxii, 79, 87, 90, 102, 112

Baier, Andrzej Ignacy (1712–85), Warmian bishop, 107
Baltic
  coast, 7, 86
  control of, 78, 87–8
  peoples, 5, 8, 12, 13, 15
  trade, 19, 86
Batory, Stefan, king of Poland, grand duke of Lithuania (1576–86), 84
Baumgarten, Siegmund Jacob (1706–57), theologian, 101
Bavaria, 25, 65, 66, 80, 91
Bayreuth (Kulmbach-), margraviate of, xx, xxiii, 24, 25, 34, 68, 84
Baysen-Bażyński, Jan von (c.1394–1459), leader of the Prussian League, 19
Berlin, xviii, xx, xxiii, 25, 29, 35, 41, 48, 49, 53, 56, 64, 66, 69–73, 76–7, 79, 93, 98, 100, 103, 104, 106, 108, 112
  Academy of Sciences in, 71, 99, 104

149

Index

Besser, Johannes von (1654–1729), Prussian ceremonial master and poet, 66–7
Bielefeld, 53
Bismarck, Otto von (1815–98), prime minister of Prussia and German chancellor, 9
Bogislav XIV, last duke of Pomerania (1625–37), 80
Bohemia, 40, 48
Borussian historiography, 2, 78, 83, 93
Brandenburg
    Electorate of, xviii, xx, xxiii, 11, 23, 25, 28, 37, 48–9, 64–5, 73, 78, 80–1, 85, 91
    guilds, 71, 102
    Kammergericht, 26–7, 69, 108
    margraves of, 11, 13, 24,
    nobility of, 30, 34–5, 43, 47–8, 53, 55–6, 59–61, 69, 72, 115
    Privy Council (1604), 26, 29, 31–2, 37, 38, 69
    Recess (1653), 49
    rural subjects, 58, 61–2, *see also* serfdom
    union with Ducal Prussia, 24, 68, 84–5
    war council, 27, 31
Breslau, 74–7, 102, 103, 106
Britain, *see* Great Britain
Bromberg (Bydgoszcz)
    treaty of (1657), 66, 87, *see* also Wehlau (Welawa)
Brunswick-Hanover, *see* Hanover

Calvinism, *see* Reformed religion
cameralism, 95, 99, 109, 114
Cammin, bishopric of, 54
Canstein, Carl Hildebrand von (1667–1719), Pietist, 100
Carlyle, Thomas (1795–1881), Scottish essayist and historian
Carmer, Johann Heinrich (1720–1801), jurist, 108
Catholicism, 65, 68, 79, 81, 82, 84, 85, 106–7, 112
    Catholics in Prussia 3, 6, 36, 37, 39, 51, 99, 101, 106, 107, 111–12

Catholic (Counter-) Reformation, 37, 39, 42
Catholic Enlightenment, 95, 107
Charles V, Holy Roman Emperor (1519–56), 26, 84, *see also* Holy Roman Empire
Charles VI, Holy Roman Emperor (1711–40), 89
Charles VII (Wittelsbach), Elector of Bavaria (1726–45), Holy Roman Emperor (1742–5), 90
Charles X Gustav, king of Sweden (1654–60), 86
Charles XII, king of Sweden (1697–1718), 67, 87–8
Charles Alexander, margrave of Brandenburg-Ansbach-Bayreuth (1757/69–91, d. 1806), 25
Charlottenburg (Lietzenburg) castle, 69
Chemnitz, Bogislav Philipp von (1605–68), historian and lawyer, 80
Christina, queen of Sweden (1632–54), 80
Cleves (Kleve), duchy of, xx, xxiii, 28, 37, 40, 44, 47–9, 51–3, 55, 69, 76, 84, 102
Cocceji, Samuel von (1679–1755), jurist, 108
Codex Carolina (1532), 26
Cölln (Berlin-), xviii, 68–9
Constantinople, 77
cordon sanitaire, 92
Cossacks, Zaporozhian, 87
Courland, xxi, xxii, 13, 85, 116
Cracow (Kraków), xxi, xxii, 20
Cujavia, xvi, 11, 14, 19

Danzig (Gdańsk), xix, xx, xxi, xxii, xxiii, 13, 16, 18, 19, 73, 76, 92
Deism, 97, 110, 111
demesne, 57–8
Denmark, 15, 35, 85–6
Dnieper, River, 88
Dohm, Christian Wilhelm (1751–1820), political and social refomer, 104

Index

Dohna, family von, 42, 60
Dohna (-Schlobitten), Abraham von (1579–1631), 42
Dorothea of Holstein-Glücksburg (1636–89), electress of Brandenburg
Draheim, xx, 56
Duchy of Prussia (also Ducal Prussia; 'East Prussia' after 1772), xix, xx, xxi, xxii, 5, 24, 25, 42, 46–7, 49–51, 55, 63, 66, 68, 73, 83–5, 92, 99, 102, 107, 113
  Brandenburg succession, 50, 84
  fief of Poland, 20, 39, 66, 84–5
  fief of Sweden, 86
  nobility, 20, 21, 27, 30, 34–5, 39, 42, 46–8, 50–1, 55–6, 59–61, 66, 67, 69, 92
  Oberrat, 42, 46
  sovereignty over, 27, 50, 65–6, 68, 86–7
  war chancery, 28
Dutch, *see* Netherlands

East Frisia, xxiii, 34, 41, 103
Edict of Nantes, Revocation of (1685), 40, 82
Eichendorff, Joseph (1788–1857), poet and novelist, 9
Elbe, River, xx, xxiii, 11, 57, 59–61, 83
Elbing (Elbląg), xix, 10, 16, 18, 73, 87
Electorate of Brandenburg, *see* Brandenburg
Elizabeth, empress of Russia (1741–62), 92
England, 66
Erlichshausen, Ludwig von, 31st grand master of the Teutonic Order (1450–67), 19
Estonia, 116
excise tax, *see Akzise*

Fehrbellin, battle of (1675), 82
Felbiger, Johann Ignaz von (1724–88), education reformer, 106
First World War, 88

France, 28, 38, 62, 66, 79, 80, 82, 86, 91, 95, 102, 103, 104, 109, 111
  armies, 98, 115
  Revolution, 110, 111, 113, 115
Francke, August Hermann (1663–1727), Pietist theologian, 98
Franconia, 24–5, 34, 68, 84
Frankfurt/Oder, 39, 99
Frederick August, Elector of Saxony, *see* Augustus the Strong
Frederick I, burgrave of Nuremberg (1397–1440), Elector of Brandenburg (1415–40), 24
Frederick II, king of Prussia (1740–86), 27, 32, 47, 56, 62–3, 64, 72–3, 75–7, 78, 83, 89–93, 95–7, 100–5, 108, 110, 112, 114–15
Frederick III/I, Elector of Brandenburg (1688–1700), king in Prussia (1701–13), 27, 32, 64–71, 83, 98, 114
Frederick V, Elector Palatine (1610–23), king of Bohemia (1619–20), 40
Frederick William, the Great Elector (1640–88), 23–4, 27–8, 30, 31–2, 36, 39–40, 47, 48–9, 51–2, 54, 64, 69–70, 79–82, 86, 87, 102
Frederick William I, king in Prussia (1713–40), 29, 33–4, 35, 47, 51, 54, 56, 65–6, 70–1, 74–5, 83, 88, 97, 99, 100, 102
Frederick William II, king of Prussia (1786–97), 72, 104, 108, 110
Frederick Wiliam III, king of Prussia (1797–1840), 113
French Revolution, *see* France

Gedike, Friedrich (1754–1803), education reformer, 112
General Directory, 29, 72, 75, 103
General War Commissariat, 28, 74
George Frederick, margrave of Ansbach (1543–1603), 25, 50, 84

Index

George William, Elector of Brandenburg, duke in Prussia (1618–40), 27, 39, 40, 79–80

Gneisenau, August Count Neidhardt von (1760–1831), Prussian field marshal, 77

Gniezno (Gnesen), bishopric of, 14

Göthe, Eosander von (1669–1728), architect and sculptor, 69

Great Britain, 79, 88, 89

Great Elector, *see* Frederick William, the Great Elector

Great Northern War (1700–21), 85, 87–8

Great Poland (Wielkopolska), xviii, xix, xxi, xxii, 19, 87, 107

Gröben, Otto von (1567–1649), 50

Grotius, Hugo (1583–1645), Dutch jurist and philosopher, 96

Grunwald, *see* Tannenberg

Guelphs (Hanoverian dynasty), 79

Gundling, Jacob Paul (1673–1731), court historian and jester, 71

Gustav Adolf, king of Sweden (1611–32), 80

Gutsherrschaft, 34, 57–63

Habsburg, house of, 9, 51, 65, 66, 79–80, 81, 86–7, 89, 90–2, 104, 107

Hague, The, 52

Halberstadt, bishopric (until 1648) and principality of, xviii, xx, 24, 48, 52–3

Halle (university of), 64, 83, 96, 97, 98, 99, 101, 111

Hanover, 65, 69, 79
  Brunswick-Hanover, 106

Hanseatic League, 15–18

Haskalah, 104

Hecker, Johann Julius (1707–68), school reformer, 100

Hegel, Georg Wilhelm Friedrich (1770–1831), philosopher, 97

Herder, Johann Gottfried (1744–1803), philosopher, 114–15

Hertzberg, Ewald Friedrich count of (1725–95), Prussian statesman, 91, 94, 115

Hobbes, Thomas (1588–1679), political philosopher, 96

Hofkammer, 29

Hohenzollern dynasty, 20, 23, 24, 25, 38, 45–8, 53–4, 65–6, 78, 82, 84, 87, 92, 93, 114–15

Holy Roman Empire, 2, 5, 6, 10, 19, 23, 35, 36, 42, 49, 52, 57, 60, 62, 71, 78–81, 82, 90–1, 98, 102, 112, 116
  Circles (*Kreise*), 31, 83, 91
  Emperor, 25, 26, 27, 37, 54, 64, 66, 80–1, 83–4, 90
  imperial defence, 31, 32, 82
  Imperial Diet, 49, 52, 91
  Imperial Law Court, 62, 83, 102
  Princes, 25, 31, 49, 65, 80–3, 91

Hoym, Carl Georg Heinrich Count von (1739–1807), Prussian minister in Silesia, 75

Huguenots, 6, 35, 40–1, 44, 82, 102, 104

Hungary, xxi, 24

ius indigenatus, 45, 50, 55, 56
ius reformandi, 36

Jadwiga, queen (monarch) of Poland (1384–99), 7

Jagiellonian (Polish) dynasty, 85

Jena and Auerstedt, battles of (1806/7), 98, 113, 117

Jesuits, 106

Jews, 3, 6, 93, 101–5, 107, 111, 112

Joachim I Nestor, Elector of Brandenburg (1499–1535), 25, 36–7

Joachim II Hector, Elector of Brandenburg (1535–71), 25, 37, 48, 49, 68, 102

Joachim Frederick, Elector of Brandenburg (1598–1608), 37

Jogaila, *see* Władysław Jagiełło

Johann Carl von Hohenzollern-Hechingen (1732–1803), bishop of Warmia, 110

Index

John, margrave of Neumark/Küstrin (1535–71), 25, 37
John George, Elector of Brandenburg (1571–98), 25, 37
John Sigismund, Elector of Brandenburg, governing duke in Prussia (1608–19), 37–8, 39, 55, 84
  Confessio Sigismundi (1614), 38–9, 69
Joseph II, Holy Roman Emperor (1765–1790), 104, 112
Jülich-Berg, 53, 84
Justi, Johann Heinrich Gottlob von (1717–71), cameralist economist and historian, 95

Kalckstein, Christian Ludwig von (1630–72), 51
Kant, Immanuel (1724–1804), philosopher, 105, 109, 111, 112, 113, 116
Kanton system, 33–4, 56, 75, 86, 100, *see also* army
Kaszubs (Kaszuby), 10, 13
Katarzyna Jagiellonka, queen of Sweden (1568–83), 85
Kettler, Gotthard, last master of the Livonian Order (1554–61) and duke of Courland (1561–87), 85
Kiev, 88
Klein, Ernst Ferdinand (1744–1810), jurist, 108
Kleist, family von, 34
Kolberg, xx, 35, 54
Kölmer (non-noble freemen), 51, 63
Komturei (also *Komtur*), 10, 12,
Königsberg, xix, xx, xxiii, 10, 16, 20, 21, 39, 49, 51, 64, 67–9, 74, 77, 80, 92, 98, 116
  University of, 84, 99, 105
Kreditwerk, 48
Krockow, family von, 55
Kulm (Chełmno), 11, 13, 15, 18, 19
  Kulm law, 12, 15, 58–9
Kulmbach-Bayreuth, *see* Bayreuth
Kulturkampf, 106

Labiau, treaty of (1656), 87
Landrat (district councillor), 46
Landtag (assembly of estates, diet), 20, 50, 63, 69
Langenberg, Nikolaus (1573–1628), 51–2
Languedoc, 62
Latvia, *see* Courland
League of Princes (1785–90), 91
League of the Rhine (1658–67), 82
Leibniz, Gottfried Wilhelm (1646–1716), philosopher and mathematician, 96–7
Leipzig, 98
Leopold I, Holy Roman Emperor (1658–1705), 27, 66
Lessing, Gotthold Ephraim (1729–81), dramatist, 104–6
Lipsius, Justus (1547–160), natural law philosopher, 36
Lithuania, grand duchy of, xix, xxi, 7, 14
  Christianisation of, 15
  Prussian Lithuania, 11, 58, 99
  union with Poland, 15, 17, 85
  see also Poland-Lithuania
Lithuanians, 10
  in Prussia, 12, 13
Livonia, xxi, xxii, 13, 85, 88, 116
London, 68, 69
Louis XIV, king of France (1643–1715), 3, 71, 80
Louis XVI, king of France (1774–1792, d. 1793), 115
Luise Henriette of Orange-Nassau (1627–67), electress of Brandenburg, 82
Lusatia, xviii, 11
Luther, Martin (1483–1546), 20, 36, 60
Lutheranism (Lutherans), 5, 35–8, 39–42, 55, 67–8, 79, 84, 98–101, 115
Lützen, 80

Magdeburg, xviii, xx, xxiii, 24, 28, 29, 35, 37, 47–8, 53–4, 76, 79, 102, 103
  Magdeburg law, 11

Index

Mainz, archbishopric of, 24, 36
Maria Theresa, Holy Roman Empress (1745–65), 89, 90, 92
Marienburg (Malbork), 9, 10, 15, 19
Mark, county of, 28, 40, 48–9, 51–2, 84
Marx, Karl (1818–83), philosopher, 92, 97
Mazovia (Mazowsze), xix, xxi, xxii, 11
Mazuria (Masuren/Mazurian lakes), 11
Melanchthon, Philipp (1497–1560), Protestant Reformer and pedagogian, 37
Memel, city of, xix, xxii, 51
 river, 11
Mendelssohn, Moses (1729–86), philosopher, 104
Mennonites, 100, 111
mercantilism, 73
Mickiewicz, Adam (1798–1855), Polish poet
Minden, duchy of, xx, 29, 47–8, 52, 53–4
Mittelmark, xviii, 48, 58
monarchomachs, 38
monarchy, 34, 38, 41, 64–77, 101, 102, 104, 107, 110, 116–17
 elevation to (1701), 8, 29, 64, 115
Monbijou palace, 71
Muscovy, 21, 85, 87, *see also* Russia
Muslims, 104

Napoleon Bonaparte, 3, 6, 9, 63, 76, 79, 113, 114, 116, 117
 Code Napoléon, 109
Nazis (National Socialists), 2, 8
Netherlands, xx, xxiii, 52, 55, 69, 82, 85, 91
 Dutch Calvinism, 38, 40
 Dutch Republic, 81
 Dutch republicanism, 51
 States General, 81
Netze District, 103, 107
Neumark, 37, 48, 56
New South Prussia (from 1793), 107

Nicolai, Friedrich (1733–1811), writer and publisher, 71, 104, 106, 111, 112
Nystad, treaty of (1721), 88, 92

Oberrat, *see* Ducal Prussia
Obertribunal (High Tribunal), 27
Oder, River, xx, xxi, xiii, 11
Oliva, monastery of, 15
Orange, house of, 69
Oranienburg castle, 69
Order of the Black Eagle, 67
Osnabrück, 54, *see also* Peace of Westphalia
Ostforschung, 9
Ottoman Empire, 21

Palatinate of the Rhine, 37
Papacy, 19, 21, 66, 84, 106
Paris, 62, 68, 95
Paul I, Emperor of Russia (1796–1801), 116
Peace of Augsburg (1555), 36, 79
Peace of Basel (1795), 116
Peace of Nijmegen (1679), 82
Peace of Prague (1635), 80
Peace of Westphalia (1648), 40, 48, 52, 65, 81, 82, 86, 87
peasant revolts of 1525, 60
Peter I, tsar of Russia (1682/96–1725), 87–8
Peter III, tsar of Russia (1762), 92
Pfalz-Neuburg, 84
Pfundgeld (or *Pfundzoll*), 17
Pietism, 6, 68, 98–101, 115
Pius II, pope (Aeneas Sylvius Piccolomini) (1458–64), 14
Poland-Lithuania, commonwealth of, xx, xxi, xxii, 3, 5, 17, 18, 27, 35, 39, 42, 44, 49–50, 55, 58, 62, 65–6, 68, 78, 79, 83–5, 87–9, 91–4, 97, 99, 102–3, 110, 116–17
 armies of, 8, 20, 35, 85, 88
 constitution of 3 May 1791, 97
 Diet (Sejm) of, 46–7, 66, 85
 law, 13, 50, 88, 92, 93, 97

154

nobility of, 12, 35, 46–7, 62, 66, 85, 88, 107
partitions of (1772, 1793, 1795), 2, 6, 20, 73, 76, 87, 89, 91, 93–4, 97, 103, 107–8, 110, 113, 116–17
trade of, 11, 19, 93
see also Great Poland; Royal (Polish Prussia); Saxony, union with Poland-Lithuania
Poles, 6, 8, 10, 13, 50, 106–8, 110, 112–13
Pöllnitz, Karl Ludwig von (1692–1775), writer and courtier, 41
Poltava, battle of (1709), 87
Pomerania
  duchy of, xviii, xix, xx, xxi, xxii, xxiii, 9, 10, 12, 54, 80, 86–7, 88
  Eastern (Prussian) Pomerania, 28–9, 35, 41, 48, 52, 54–5, 73, 102, 107
  nobility, 35–6, 47, 54
  Swedish Pomerania, xx, 52, 55 80, 85, 86, 88
Pomerelia (Polish Pomerania, Pomorze), 13, 19, 87
Poniatowski, Stanisław August, last king of Poland (1764–95, d. 1798), 92
Posilge, Johann von (1340–1418), chronicler and priest, 15
Potsdam, 69, 70, 71, 72, 74, 76
  cabinet in, 72
  Edict of Potsdam (1685), 40
  Treaty of (1719), 88
Poznań, xvii, xx, xxii, xxiii, 19
Pragmatic Sanction, 89
Prätorius, Matthäus (1635–1707), historian, 13
Prignitz, 4, 48
Prussian League (1440–53), 16–17, 19
Pruzzen, 10, 11, 12, 14, 57–8, 84
Pufendorf, Samuel von (1632–94), jurist, political philosopher and historian, 96

Ranke, Leopold von (1795–1886), historian, 97

Ravensberg, xx, 47–8, 51, 53
Reformation, Protestant 12, 21, 26, 36–8, 79
  Second Reformation, 38, 55
Reformed religion (Calvinism), 5, 35, 36–9, 40–2, 55–6, 60, 67–8, 79, 82
  see also Huguenots; Netherlands, Dutch Calvinism
Regensburg, 52
Régie, 75
Regimentsnottel, 50
Renaissance, 14, 17
Rétablissment, 99
Rhine, 53, 69, 109
Rhineland, 41
Rome, 15, 25, 66
Royal (Polish) Prussia, xxii, xxiii, 44, 73–4, 76, 79, 86, 87, 91–3, 103, 107
  incorporation into the Polish crown, 19–20, 21
  West Prussia, 93, 97, 98, 103, 113, 116
  see also Poland-Lithuania, partitions of
Rügen, island of, 88
Russia, 62, 79, 87–8, 91–2, 94, 116, *see also* Muscovy

Salic Law, 89
Salzburg, 100
Savoy, 65
Saxony, Electorate of, xviii, 35, 36, 54, 65, 66, 70, 79, 80, 89, 90, 95
  union with Poland, 65, 90
Scharnhorst, Gerhard von (1755–1813), chief of general staff, 77
Schlüter, Andreas (1659–1714), sculptor and architect, 69
Schmalkaldic League (1530–47), 37
Schwarzenberg, Adam von (1583–1641), Brandenburg-Prussian minister, 27, 40, 79, 80
Schwerin, Otto von (1616–79), Brandenburg-Prussian diplomat, 50–1, 70

Index

Second Northern War (1655–60), 28, 32, 49, 85–7
serfdom, 12, 43, 50–60, 57–61
Seven Years War (1756–63), 35, 63, 74, 76, 89–90, 92, 114, 116
Sienkiewicz, Henryk (1846–1916), Polish novelist, 9
Sigismund I, the 'Old', king of Poland, grand duke of Lithuania (1506–48), 20–1
Sigismund III Vasa, king of Sweden (1592–99), king of Poland and grand duke of Lithuania (1587–1632), 42, 50, 85
Sigismund of Hohenzollern (1538–66), archbishop of Magdeburg, son of Joachim II, 53
Silesia, xxi, xxii, xxiii, 9, 24, 34, 41, 48, 72, 75, 79, 83, 89–91, 101, 102–3, 112
    Upper Silesia, 106–7
Smolensk, 88
social militarisation, theory of, 5, 73, 75
Society of Jesus, *see* Jesuits
Sonderweg, 2, 5, 59, 61, 73
Sophie Charlotte of Hanover, queen in Prussia (1701–5), consort of Frederick III/I, 69, 71
Sound (tolls), 86
Spain, crown of, 65
Spanish War of Succession (1701–14), 66
Spener, Philip Jakob (1635–1705), Pietist theologian, 98
Speyer, 83
Spree, River, 68
Ständestaat ('state of estates'), 20, 22–3, 32–33, 39, 47–8, 57
Stettin, 88, 103
Stockholm, 70
Suarez, Carl Gottlieb (1746–98), jurist, 108
Swabia, Upper, 62
Sweden, 49, 52, 53, 55, 67, 70, 78–80, 85–8
    army of, 27, 32, 34, 35
    Swedish Deluge (wars of the), 87

table of precedence (court ranks), 69, 70
Tacitus, Publius Cornelius, Roman historian (56–117), 15
Tagfahrten, 17
Tannenberg, battle of (1410), 7, 8, 10, 15
Tatars, 21, 89
Teutonic Order (also Teutonic Knights), 5, 7–10, 12, 14–18, 19–20, 49, 93
    castles of, 7, 9, 10, 12
    chronicles, 14
    cities, 16–18
    grand master of, 7, 11, 18, 19, 21, 24
    military, 12, 17, 21
    nobility, 14–16, 50
    secularisation, 5, 7, 19–21, 36, 84
Thirteen Years War (1454–66), 13, 19
Thirty Years War (1618–48), 22, 27, 31, 35, 39, 54, 79, 86, 98
Thomasius, Christian (1655–1728), theologian and political philosopher, 96
Thorn (Toruń), xx, xxi, xxii, xxiii, 15, 16, 18, 19, 73
    Colloquy of (1645), 39
Tobacco College, 71
Toland, John (1670–1722), political writer and freethinker, 69
Treitschke, Heinrich (1834–96), nationalist historian, 9
Tridentine Council (Council of Trent, 1545–63), 37
Tuscany, 65

Uckermark, xviii, 4, 48, 59, 61
Unification of Germany (1871), 1, 2, 78
Upper Silesia, *see* Silesia

Venice, 65
Versailles, 70, 71
Vienna, 62, 68
Vistula, River, xx, xxiii, 14, 92
Voltaire (1694–1778), French philosopher and satirist, 85, 110
Vytautas, *see* Witold

Index

Waldeck, Georg von (1620–92), field marshal and minister, 28
Wallenstein, Albrecht von (1583–1634), imperial military leader, 80
Warmia (Ermland), bishopric of, xix, 11, 19, 107
Warsaw (Warszawa), xxi, xxii, xxiii, 39, 46, 51, 85, 87
Wehlau (Welawa), treaty of 1657, 66, 8, *see also* Bydgoszcz (Bromberg)
Westforschung, 9
Westphalia, 34, 52, 53, 75, *see also* Peace of Westphalia
West Prussia, *see* Royal (Polish) Prussia
Wettin (Saxon house of), 65, 79
Wetzlar, 83
Wilich von Winnenthal, Dietrich Karl, 52
William II, German Emperor (1888–1918, d. 1941), 9

Witold (Vytautas), grand duke of Lithuania (1392/1401–30), 7
Wittenberg, 37, 39
Władysław IV, Wasa, king of Poland and grand duke of Lithuania (1632–48), 39
Władysław Jagiełło (Jogaila), grand duke of Lithuania (1377–1434), king of Poland (1386/99–1434), 7, 15
Włocławek (Leslau), bishopric of, 14
Wolff, Christian (1679–1754), philosopher, 6, 67, 96, 97, 99, 101, 110
Wöllner, Johann Christoph (1732–1800), minister, 110–11
Wusterhausen castle, 72

Zinsbauern, 11
Zips (Spisz), 92